HOLY ANGELS - MAL'A

(God Has Commanded His Holy Angels to Guard You in All Your Ways, Ps 91:11)

NIHIL OBSTAT
Rev Fr. Christian Amogu
December 18, 2012

Imprimatur
+Paulinus C. Ezeokafor
December 18, 2012

Order this book online at www.trafford.com
or email orders@trafford.com

Most Trafford titles are also available at major online book retailers.

Printed in the United States of America.

ISBN: 978-1-4907-1354-0 (sc)
ISBN: 978-1-4907-1353-3 (e)

Trafford rev. 09/03/2013

 www.trafford.com

North America & international
toll-free: 1 888 232 4444 (USA & Canada)
fax: 812 355 4082

DEDICATED TO

MY GUARDIAN ANGELS (*human* and *Spiritual*)

FOR THEIR LOVE AND PROTECTION.

ACKNOWLEDGMENT

I wish I could live the rest of my life as a thanksgiving to the Almighty God for the unmerited favour He granted me in the process of this publication. But I will always thank Him with every breath that issues from my nostrils for rest of my life, He deserves it. I am grateful to all who contributed directly and indirectly to this work. To my Bishops, Most Rev Dr S. A. Okafor (emeritus), Most Rev Dr. P. C. Ezeokafor (the incumbent) and Most Rev Dr. S. A. Amatu (my God-Father and Bishop of Okigwe) I remain ever grateful for your contributions in my formation and sustenance.

I remember with love and gratitude my late parents Mr and Mrs D. O. Anokwulu and simply commend you in the loving hands of the Holy Angels. I am grateful to all my siblings and entire Anokwulu family for all we share together, especially my twin sister, Rev Sr. Schola Anokwulu.

I remember with special affection those '*human Angels*' whom God has place on my path to assist me in various capacities; Eduardo and AnnaMaria Ciampa, Msgr. Steven R. Camp, and Don Antonio Precchia you are angels that I can see with physical eyes.

I had inspirations, companionship and support from a lot of friends both clerics, religious and lay people. I cannot mention all here save for few that are outstanding; Frs. Charles Okoye, Fabian Obi, JonasBesnson Okoye, Toni Akabuogu, Poly Nnajiofo, John Umeojiako and Celestine Ekwueme. Others, Rev Frs Ejike Mbaka, P. Chukwukebe, J. O. Umeh, C. Okonkwo, H. Nwamadu, B. Ezemadubom, F. Oranefo and host of others, may God sustain you in His vineyard. Others who are not priests but made me realize the existence of Angels; Bontus, Cynthia, Ebere, Adaobi, Chinwe, Nkemjika and Ifeoma, may you remain in the care of the Holy Angels.

I cannot forget those who worked on the manuscript in many ways, Fr Christian Amogu, my brother Jude Okpala, and others, thanks for your prompt and quick assistance. I really thank everybody dear to me and pray that your holy Angels guard you onto eternal life for me.

HOLY ANGELS
The Mal'ak Elohim

(God has commanded His Holy Angels Concerning You to Guard You in All Your Ways, Ps 91:11)

Foreword

To be sure, those who do not believe in the existence and activity of the holy Angels will have a hard time with all this. But whoever takes his Faith in the Church's teaching on the Angels seriously will find the evidence for the existence and activity of the holy Angels throughout Sacred Scripture, from Genesis to the Apocalypse. The Lord's coming is always preceded by the holy Angels, whether it is His coming in the flesh (Lk 1,26) or His second coming in glory (Mt 25, 31; Lk 9, 26: Apoc 22,6). From the Acts of the Apostles we see clearly that for the first Christians, faith in the Holy Angels and the experience of their intervention was a reality beyond question (cf. e.g. Acts 12, 15). For the saints throughout the history of the Church the existence of these powerful, pure spirits was a truth of faith quite concrete, which they could experience for themselves time and again. A great many saints were united in a very special manner to the Angels, above all to their Guardian Angels, by means of an extraordinary veneration and love, at times even by means of a unique familiarity with them.

("Opus Sanctorum Angelorum" 1997), Fr. Benoit Duroux, O.P.

Catecheses on the holy angels are not new in the Catholic Tradition, and they are founded on the belief and acceptance that the whole creation is under the guidance of a supreme and invisible God, who multiplies His power through the angels, Mal'ak Elohim. The Lateran Council (1215) and Vatican Council I (1869), among others, upheld that belief. Karl Rahner shares the same sentiment about the existence of angel: "existence of the angels cannot be disputed by a sincere Christian. They are mere creatures, and like man, they are created for a supernatural goal. Their saving grace came from Christ, who is their Head too, and around the Word, they form a true society of persons. They are a part of the Christian Message." Pope John Paul II followed suit in an eloquent catecheses in July-August 1989, detailing the whole gamut of the nature of the holy angels in divine Revelation and based on the Holy Scripture, the Tradition, and the teachings of the Church. Even before him, Pope Pius XII urged us to "unite" and form a "family" with the angels. In *Humani Generis* (1950), he denounced theologians who were drifting away from such teachings.

Mal'ak Elohim participates in this tradition of catecheses on the holy angles and automatically verifies its authenticity. One can see that participation in the first part, which is mainly a biblical exegesis on the existence and activities of the holy angels, their nature, ranks, ministries, and divine commands. From those discussions, *Mal' ak Elohim* reiterates the good services the holy angels perform. It traces these services to the observations of the Church Fathers, the Holy Scripture, and lives of saints. In those regards, Fr. Sebastian Anokwulu is

8

eclectic; there is a superabundance of evidence to use, but the gist of the services of the angels still resounds in what he presents:

- They protect us from evil.
- They defend us against the temptations of the evil spirits.
- They protect us when we are in danger.
- They inspire holy thoughts.
- They guide us.

The second part details the activities of the angels in the lives of people of God and instantiates their good services. Every account rendered in this part borders on imaginative excesses, yet they inscribe clear notion of Catholic faith that is the *conditio sine qua non* for understanding them. What is rather critical is the discussion of the manifestations of evil spirit, which is a counterpoint to the holy angels. The discussion is, rather, crucial to the text because of what Fr. Anokwulu deems scarcity of communion with the holy angels. It would not be unreasonable to expose metaphysical and theological abstractions implied in the discussion: Evil spirit is a real entity; evil spirit transcends space and time; evil spirit can inhabit anyone who has lost the light of God, especially as revealed through His Son; evil spirit has power to prevent one from the beatific vision. Accordingly, the issue is not the reality of evil spirits. The catechism affirms their reality and calls them "Satan," with a leadership in Lucifer. Pope John Paul II addressed that elaborately in his 1989 catecheses:

> The choice made on the basis of the truth about God, known in a higher way because of the clarity of their intellects, has divided also the world of pure spirits into the good and the bad. The good chose God as the supreme and definitive Good, known to the intellect enlightened by Revelation. To have chosen God means that they turned to him with all the interior force of their freedom, a force which is love. God became the total and definitive scope of their spiritual existence. The others instead turned their backs on God contrary to the truth of the knowledge which indicated him as the total and definitive good. Their choice ran counter to the revelation of the mystery of God, to his grace which made them partakers of the Trinity and of the eternal friendship with God in communion with him through love. On the basis of their created freedom they made a radical and irreversible choice on a parity with that of the good angels, but diametrically opposed. Instead of accepting a God full of love they rejected him, inspired by a false sense of, self-sufficiency, of aversion and even of hatred which is changed into rebellion.

Yet, the power of the evil spirits is useless without our abysmal use of freedom. We provide agency for evil spirits by deviating in our path, especially when we occupy ourselves with mundane appetites and privilege destructive desires. This occupation is a form of violence, not an objective and physical one; it does not necessarily bring about war, but a system of thought that has to be in place for the appetites and desires to be acceptable and satisfied.

The personal narratives in the second part point at this use of freedom that brings about the opposition between good and evil. As personal narratives, this part of the text invites literary scrutiny. Who is telling the story? From whose perspective is the story told? The relative complexity of the narratives undermines clear answers, but one cannot become oblivious of the distinction between the story-time and the narrative-time. The narrative, naturally, reconstructs the story and presents it for a specific purpose. The satisfaction of this purpose is always intentional and collides with "hermeneutics temptations": the desire to make sense. Fr. Anokwulu is recapitulating his memory from a physical time and place, and, as such, becomes a victim of language through which, only, he can share that memory. By sharing, he calls up his vulnerability and invites throes of psychoanalytical queries; by sharing, also, he searches for deeper meaning in the narratives; equally by sharing, he wants us to think about the relationship between "(factual) truth and truthfulness." What he narrates violates logical norms of any speech community. Yet, to use Slavoj Zizek, his truthfulness lies in his "very factual unreliability, its confusion, its inconsistency. . . . the very factual deficiencies . . . bear witness to the truthfulness . . . since they [deficiencies] signal that the reported content 'contaminated' the manner of reporting." In other words, he cannot tell of his experiences without gaps and flaws and without inciting doubt. What is more important is not the order of facts in his personal narratives, but what the story and experiences have awakened in him. By telling, therefore, he accepts the responsibility that came with the experiences. There is an ethics there: what do you do with what you know?

The narrative of the encounter with the "professional"—an evil spirit who took possession of Fr. Anokwulu's cousin – details this ethics. The "professional" was intransigent, and he boasted his power with relative recklessness and even to the point of diffusing Fr. Anokwulu's armada of spiritual pinions. But not until he invoked Mary, Mother of God, the Queen of the angels. The "professional" recoiled in fear and desolation at the mention of Her name. That exemplary devotion is what *Mal' ak Elohim* calls for, and he uses "slavery" to describe that devotion—recognition of the power of faith in abandoning oneself to divinity. Faith is illuminated as that which makes possible what is reasonably impossible; it is a mode of knowing and understanding the world that requires piety. Accordingly, evil spirit is a limited being; his power is limited, and it atrophies in the presence of Christ.

Mal' ak Elohim brings us back to how we ought to relate with the holy angels, whom God created as his messengers. It motivates us to live up to our faith without trepidation. It urges us to get familiar with them fully according to divine ordination, for every one of us, at the moment of conception, has a divinely chosen angel. It will not be amiss to resort to the suggestion outlined in this observation attributed to Pope Pius XII:

> In speaking with someone who is closed to your argument, go to your guardian angel and recommend the matter to him. Ask him to take it up with the guardian angel of the person you have to see. Once the two angels establish an understanding, the conversation with the visitor will be much easier.

A similar remark is an exhortation of St. Bernard of Clairvaux: "My brothers, make the holy angels your friends. Give them joy by having confidential recourse to them, and honor them by your prayers, for they are ever near, to comfort and protect you." Put simply, the holy angels are acolytes of our will, and are integral to the salvation of souls through the Resurrection of Christ.

This brings me back to the starting point, the observation by Fr. Benoit Duroux, O.P. Anyone who does not believe harbors a challenge to offer alternative explanation, for what makes that doubt conducive is neither knowledge nor even the proximity of knowledge, but a frailty of thought and narrow vision that, at best, will pose logical and philosophical refutations. The reality of angels is not a matter of Socratic examination; even when that is admirably useful, it is still insufficient as the epistemic mode for understanding reality that operates independently of matter. Indeed, philosophical uses of reason are not opposed to Revealed Truth: certain phenomena in our reality are self-evident; others require a leap of faith; and they all point to one Truth. "Eye has not seen, nor ear heard, neither have entered the hearts of men, the thing which God prepared for those who love Him" (1 Cor. 2: 9). And that transcendent bounty is integral to what God does among us with and through the holy angels.

Jude Chudi Okpala
Walden University, USA.

11

GENERAL INTRODUCTION

After my priestly ordination in 1994, I have had many occasions where my pastoral duty exposed me to the spiritual difficulties many people express concerning evil spirits – demons. Very rarely do I encounter someone talking about good spirits – I mean, the Angels. I do not doubt the reality and truths about the presence and works of these evil forces but obviously in most cases, they are exaggerated. Indeed, fears of these evil forces create more problems for many of the people I have met than does the evil spirits themselves. Many individuals, many families, and various areas of business, career and undertakings seem continually harassed by the fear of demons. Thus, many people resort to anything, anybody or any place that offers immediate succor to this fear. I have always personally wondered why the good spirits – the Angels – make no such impact on people like the demons.

Hence, when I had the opportunity to specialize in Biblical Theology in 2006 (after 12 years of pastoral encounters) I developed the interest to study the reality of the Angels in the Holy Scriptures with the intention of rediscovering for the faithful the ministry and the presence of these Angels in their daily lives. When I made up my mind to write my findings, I was aware of the difficulty surrounding writing on the subject matter of the Angels.

I knew that the nature of the work I am undertaking lends itself on the threshold of mystery. When Manoah asked the Angel that visited him his name, the Angel replied, "It is *a mystery*" (cf. Jdg. 13:18). With the indefinite article '*a*', it does not seem that the Angel identified himself as *mystery*. He only points to Manoah the nature of his name - his name is '*a mystery*'. This correlates to the answer Moses received from God in Ex. 3:14 on the proper name of God. Thus, the subject matter of the Angels borders on the doorstep of the revelation of the mystery of God. Although my interest in this work is not to study properly the *essence* or the *nature* of the angels, but their *ministry* to man, even at that, one has to acknowledge that the undertaking is a difficult one because scripturally, the appearances and operations of the Angels are intertwined with the mystery of God Himself.[1] Angels are not treated in isolation from God. God's revelation never aims at informing us regarding the nature of Angels. When and wherever they are mentioned in the Bible, it is always in order to inform us further about God, what God does, and how He does it.

Another difficulty I must acknowledge is that, on the subject matter of Angels, we do not have many writings by local authors as in other areas. In fact, the subject seems to be a neglected area of study by spiritual writers in general.[2] This notwithstanding, the doctrine of Angels holds an important place in the Word of God for Catholics and indeed for Christians in general. While there is abundant mention of Angels in the Bible, the nature of this revelation is without the same kind of explicit description, which we often find with other subjects developed in the Bible. Although recently, as I read from an article in a quarterly published by Dallas Theological Seminary[3], "we have been bombarded... by what could easily be called *Angelmania*", that is, a widespread discussion and interest on the topic of Angels, the majority of these discussions is not rooted in the Scriptures, religious or ecclesial traditions.

Hence, anyone who picks the interest to study works on the Angels as I do would have to be cautioned on falling into two extreme errors[4]: first are the rationalists that group angels and demons together as personification of psychological realities and would like to see in these realities only a mythical interpretation that psychoanalysis would provide. The other extreme, reactionary to the first, are the spiritualists with lively interest in the invisible world, who by all kinds of spiritism, would like to penetrate into the unknown, imprudently straying from the access way given to us in Christ - the Holy Bible.

---

[1] Divine theophanies most often were in the form of angelic appearances. Confer *mal'ak haelohim* in the *Elohists'* account of: Gn 21:17; 31:11 Ex 14:19, Jdg 6:20; 13:6; 13:9; or *mal'ak Yahweh* in the *Jahwists'* account of: Gn 16:7; 16:9; 16:10; 16:11; 22:11; 22:15 Ex 3:2 Nu 22:22- 27; 22:31- 35 and in Jdg 2:1; 2:4 5:23 6:11; 6:21- 22; 13:3; 13:13- 18; 13:20; 13:20; 13:21.

[2] Millard J. Erickson, *Christian Theology*, Baker Book House, Grand Rapids, 1983, p.434; Ryrie holds similar opinion when he writes that, "One has only to peruse the amount of space devoted to angelology in standard theologies to demonstrate this. This disregard for the doctrine may simply be neglect or it may indicate a tacit rejection of this area of biblical teaching. Even Calvin was cautious in discussing this subject" (*Institutes*, I, xiv, 3). Cf. Charles C. Ryrie, *Basic Theology*, Victor Books, Wheaton, IL, 1987, chapter 17, electronic media.

[3] Cf. "Kindred Spirit," a magazine published quarterly by Dallas Theological Seminary, Summer 1995, pp. 5-7.

[4] J., DANIELOU, *The Angels and Their Mission, according to the Fathers of the Church*, Texas: Christian Classics, 1957, p. vii.

My personal search in this study is to rediscover through the Holy Scriptures the truths about the angels and their mission. It is a worthwhile venture in spite of the difficulties as the French Jesuit theologian, Father Jean Danielou concludes: "… it will not be inopportune to speak of the angels…the greatest among the saints and the men of God, from St. Augustine to John Henry Newman, have always lived on familiar terms with them. And the tradition of the Church has always accorded them a place in her theology."[5]

Having worked as a diocesan Catholic Priest among the Igbos of the Eastern Nigeria, I can without scientific statistics estimate that more than 60% of our Christians (across all denomination and especially among the less literate) believe that inexplicable difficulties in their lives are caused by evil spirits. I found myself in continuous difficulty trying to explain and reassure the faithful I encounter that even though these forces exist, their presence is amplified because of the absence of the good spirits – the Angels – in their belief system. Here is an imagery: imagine a situation where the electric light is off at night and a night rodent (a rat) begins to search for food in the house of a woman who has always been tormented by the fear of witches or demons, and she has no ready torch-light or electricity to switch on. Think of how much nerve-jangling the movement of a house rat would cause this woman in a room without a bright light. In the darkness of the room, a simple house rat could take the phantom of a ghost and torment the inmate psychologically, physically, and spiritually till the day brakes. But supposing this woman has ready electric light to switch on in the room or a handy touch-light to flash at the instant of the rat's entrance, she would have been spared the stress-filled night waiting for the dawn. What this imagery goes to conclude is that, in the absence of *Light*, **darkness** can be ominously terrible to a person.

Therefore, my little effort in this booklet, using the instance of Peter's experience in Acts 12:5-11, is to attempt to **_rediscover_** and **_indicate_** the switch for the Light of the Angels for my people in particular and all Christian faithful in general who are tortured by fear of demons: '**_Rediscover_**', because the truth about the Angels' presence and ministry to man has already been revealed to us in the Scriptures; '**_Indicate_**', because like the Apostle Peter (Acts, 12: 5-11),[6] in

---

[5] Ibid. p. viii.
[6] New Revised Standard Version (NRSV) *Acts 12:5-11 While Peter was kept in prison, the church prayed fervently to God for him. [6] The very night before Herod was going to bring him out, Peter, bound with two chains, was sleeping between two soldiers, while guards in front of the door were keeping watch over the prison. [7] Suddenly an*

moments of spiritual imprisonment with fear of the evil forces, one may need an intervening direction from an Angel to:

First, "*flood our cell with heavenly light…*" (v.7): that is, to bring us into a divine presence and illumine our minds and spirit.

Second, "*tap on us…*" (v.7): that is, wake us up from our stupor and fate-resignation; and

Third, help us to "*fasten our belt… put on our sandals…wrap on our cloak and follow…*" (v.8): on to the joy and realization that "*Now I am sure that the Lord has sent his Angel and rescued me…*" (v.11).

I am fully convinced that if the evil forces are at work in the natural and human realm, the Angels or the Good Spirits are more potently at work on the same realm. Which of them should have our interest and attention? The Angels! In the presence of bright Light, there could be no darkness! If the reader becomes aware of this reality through this work, then to the glory of God, new light is shinning to the dispersion of darkness and its ominous agents.

The first part of the work outlines the Scriptural foundation of the Angels. These are interspersed with instances of exegetical connections and theological interpretations based on Catholic tradition to give different parts of a Scriptural verse a read-through. The second part outlines the ministry of the Angels with the intention of reviving the readers' faith and devotion to these heavenly friends. May the help of my Guardian Angel and the Angels of communication see me through this task. Amen!

---

*angel of the Lord appeared and **a light shone in the cell**. **He tapped Peter** on the side and woke him, saying, "Get up quickly." And the chains fell off his wrists.* [8] *The angel said to him, "**Fasten your belt and put on your sandals**." He did so. Then he said to him, "**Wrap your cloak around you and follow me**."* [9] *Peter went out and followed him; he did not realize that what was happening with the angel's help was real; he thought he was seeing a vision.* [10] *After they had passed the first and the second guard, they came before the iron gate leading into the city. It opened for them of its own accord, and they went outside and walked along a lane, when suddenly the angel left him.* [11] *Then Peter came to himself and said, "Now I am sure that the Lord has sent his angel and rescued me from the hands of Herod and from all that the Jewish people were expecting."*

CHAPTER ONE

THE ANGELS – 'MAL'AKIM ELOHIM'

1.1 INTRODUCTION

One expects the reader would be eager to be introduced immediately to discover the mysteries of the Angels as contained in the Scriptures. Instead, we will proceed naturally from the known facts to areas only faith and the Holy Spirit can help us understand better. Thus, the first chapter will aim to understand the biblical origins of the terms associated with Angels. This is important for two reasons: First, to make the connection between Old Testament and New Testament uses of certain terms clear. Second, to define the origins of the kind of 'Angels' we are discussing in this work. We will begin from the root of the commonest English appellation 'Angel'.

1.2 ORIGIN OF THE ENGLISH TERM 'ANGEL'

Biblically, the English word "angel" comes from the Latin "angelus" (which itself derives from the ancient Greek term "angelos" or "'aggelos"), meaning 'a messenger' or 'one who is sent on a mission'. Peter Llyod provides us with credible reason for this Greek origin because one would ordinarily expect the root of 'angel' biblically to come from either Hebrew (OT language) or Aramaic (the vernacular used by Jesus during His earthly life). Its Greek origin, as Llyod explained, is because Greek was the language of the Hellenistic intelligentsia among whom St Paul's epistles (which were foundation of Christianity as we know it) first vigorously spread. This Greek word "angelos" was therefore used in the early Christian era to translate the Hebrew word "mal'akh", which could mean 'a messenger' or 'an agent', and which in turn comes from the Hebrew verb 'malakha", meaning 'to toil or work', from the root "lakh", meaning 'mission' or 'service'.

To put the above explanation in a simpler expression, the word '*Angel*' is the English rendering of the Latin '*Angelus*' which was translated from the Greek '*Angelos*'. This Greek word was itself a translation of Hebrew "*Mal'ak elohim*". *Mal'ak elohim*, as we would see, means "a messenger of God"[7]. The English translations of the Scripture are replete with these words "Angel" or "Angels".[8] In a general sense, the word either in singular or plural, always refers to divine messengers. To understand the origins better, we briefly outline the connection between the OT *Mal'ak elohim* and the NT *Angel*.

1.3 THE CONNECTION BETWEEN 'MAL'AK ELOHIM' OF THE OT AND THE 'ANGELUS' OF THE VULGATE.

In the OT, the word *Mal'ak* (*messenger*) occurred 213 times referring to "messengers" or "envoys"[9] sent to carry out orders from *Divine* or *human* 'Sender'. In all the OT occurrences, two points are characteristically notable about these messengers: first, they are not responsible or answerable to themselves but rather dependent on the will of the one who sends them; and secondly, they could be human or divine (meaning respectively sent by man or by God). Divine messengers are those sent by God from heaven while human messengers are sent by earthly chieftains:

> The mal'ak does not report his own message; his function and message
> are dependent upon the will of the person who sends him. His
> significance derives not from who he is, but from who his superior is.[10]

To make their distinction and significance sharper, it would be good to give instances of OT *human* and *divine* Messengers.

---

[7] K., GERHARD, et al., *The Theological Dictionary of the New Testament* (TDNT), Grand Rapids, MI: Wm. B. Eerdmans Publishing Company, 2000.

[8] In the NRSV we are quoting, they appeared 237x and 103x respectively.

[9] M., FREEDMAN, et al. (eds), *The Theological Dictionary of the Old Testament* (TDOT), vol. XIII, p.308.

[10] Ibid. p. 309.

1.3.1   OT Human Messengers (Mal'akim)

First of all, remember that in using the terms *Human* or *Divine messengers* in this write-up, we do not mean a messenger(s) in human form or divine form but rather messenger(s) sent by human authority or divine authority. In other words, it is the authority sending the messenger that defines the agency rather than the agent himself.

In the OT, *mal'ak* referring to human messengers occurred 92 times.[11] Out of these 92x, only 4 of them refers to '*Personal envoys*',[12] while 88 refers to '*Political envoys*'. [13] An example of personal envoys could be found in Gen. 32: 4, 7 where Jacob sends *mal'akim* to Esau to announce his home return. They carried the message of peace and reconciliation to Esau. On the other hand, the use of *Political envoy* (*mal'ak*)[14] or *Political envoys* (*mal'akim*) was more common, as one can see from the number of its occurrence. Their mission included communication between citizens (1Sam. 6:21), between kings (2Sam. 5:11), between generals of an army (2Sam. 3:26) and other administrative and military personnel. We are not going into the details of their mode of errands. Our major concern here is to indicate that there existed in the OT human messengers that used the same word (*mal'akim*) as divine messengers.

1.3.2   OT Divine Messengers (*Mal'akim*)

Unlike the case of human messengers discussed above, the term *mal'ak* signifying *divine messenger* in the singular occurred (120 times) more than the plural *mal'akim* – messengers. Out of the 120 occurrences of *mal'ak* as an envoy of God, only 15 occurred in plural forms.[15] The reason is: "*A messenger of God is one whose message originates from and is sent by God ... God sends his heavenly and earthly envoys one by one; a plurality of messengers is not necessary, since God himself protects both his messengers and his message* (cf. Jer. 1:7f)".[16] In the OT,

---

[11] Ibid. p. 311.

[12] Prov. 13:17; Job. 1:14; Gen. 32: 4, 7(3,6).

[13] 16x in singular and 72x in plural. The abundance of the plural forms attests the common political practice of sending more than one messengers for security reasons. Their mission was both within the State (Cf. Josh. 7:22; 1Sam. 6:21) and Inter State (Cf. Jgs. 11:17; 2Sam. 5:11; 1Kgs. 16:7; 17:4; 19:9).

[14] 1Sam. 23:27; 2Sam. 11:19, 22:23, 25; 2Kgs. 9:18; 10:8; 2Chr. 18:12.

[15] M., FREEDMAN, et al.(eds), *TDOT*, vol. XIII, Op. Cit., p.315.

[16] Loc. Cit.

three categories of divine messengers were designated by the same term *mal'ak*. These include; prophets, priests and *mal'ak elohim* (angels).

In the case of the prophets,[17] Haggai for instance is designated as both a *nabi'* (a prophet, cf. 1:3) and a *mal'ak YHWH* (a messenger of Yahweh, cf. 1:13). The reason is because every true prophet is a messenger sent by God to his people.[18] In the plural form too, *mal'akim* refers to prophets.[19] In fact, the title *nabi'* is reserved for those who function as *mal'ak*.[20]

The word commonly used for priests in the OT is *kohen* but in two instances the word *mal'ak* was used for priests.[21] The same reason is obvious; the role of a priest is both to deliver the message (*mal'ak*) of God as a teacher of the torah, and to guard (*kohen*) this message.

Finally, the third category is our major focus of interest: the *mal'ak elohim or mal'ak YHWH*. "These two phrases are construct chains occurring 10 and 56 times respectively."[22] But precisely in 24 instances, the term refers to "the angel of God".[23] We would look into the details of these occurrences when we discuss them according to their ranks and ministry. But for now what is the connection between these OT occurrences and the Vulgate?

The Septuagint,[24] following the Classical Greek usage makes no distinction between the human and divine messengers in translating *mal'ak* from the Hebrew to Greek. In general, it translates all to *ángelos*. Whereas the Latin rendering of this translation in the Vulgate distinguishes between *nuntius* (a messenger sent by man) and *angelus* (one sent by God).[25] Thus, the English translation from the Vulgate follows the distinction making the references clearer than the Septuagint. However, this back grounding is to help the reader to understand that when

---

[17] The designation *mal'ak* is parallel to *nabi'* which occurred once in the singular and 4 times in the plural.

[18] "For you shall go to all to whom I send you, and you shall speak whatever I command you" (Jer. 1, 7).

[19] Cf. 2Chr. 36:15f; Is. 44:26; Ezk. 30:9.

[20] M. FREEDMAN, Op. Cit., p. 316.

[21] Cf. Mal. 2: 6 and Eccl. 4: 17-5, 6.

[22] M. FREEDMAN, Op. Cit., p. 317.

[23] Loc. cit.: The areas of concentrations in the angel references are: Gen. 16: 22; Ex. 23: 32, 33; Num. 22; Judg 2; Judg. 6:13; 2Sam. 24; 1Chr. 21; 1Kg. 19: 2; Is. 37; 2Chr. 32; Zach. 1-6, 12; Mal. 2:3.

[24] The Septuagint or LXX refers to the Greek translation of the Old Testament writings used by the Jewish Hellenes (Jews who lived in Greek world and could no longer read Hebrew language well). The translation which was believed to have been done by seventy Jewish scholars earned it the name 'Septuagint' or 'LXX'.

[25] M., FREEDMAN, Op. Cit., p. 309.

the term angel(s) is used in this work, one has to bear in mind that we are referring to *angelus* (*angeli*) – messenger(s) sent by God for a mission.

CHAPTER TWO

WHO ARE THE ANGELS – *MAL'AKIM ELOHIM*?

The existence of Angels is a truth of faith. Believers could better appreciate this truth. The traditional Catholic Catechism describes Angels as "spiritual non-corporal beings… who surrounds God".[26] To answer the question "who are they?" is to discuss their nature and existence. The witness of the Scriptures and the testimony of the Fathers of our faith (what in Catholic faith we call Tradition) are clear enough for a Believer. As shown in the first chapter, Saint Augustine said that when one uses the name 'Angel', he is referring to the 'office' or 'mission' or 'ministry' of these Holy Beings. But if one wants to know their nature, it is 'spirit'.[27] My major interest in this work focuses on the *ministry* of the Holy Angels not on the *nature* of their existence

However, it would be a huge presumption not to provide evidences in the Scriptures witnessing to the nature of their existence. The mission of the Holy Angels, their ministry presupposes their existence. The Bible has many instances of these presuppositions. Before we get into that, remember that throughout this work, any mention of *Angels* has to be taken as the "holy" ones unless otherwise indicated. For in general, the nuances of Angels include both pre-biblical conceptions of messengers of gods.[28] Thus there are many types of angels according to world religions. In ordinary parlance too, we have vogues like: "angel of darkness", "angel of death", "angel of misfortune", etc. Our text is concerned, as explained earlier, with the "holy angels of the Lord" (*ma'lakim elohim*).

---

[26]Cf. Pss 115:16; 19:2; Mt 5:16; The Catechism of the Catholic Church (CCC), no. 326-336.

[27] St. Augustine, En. in Ps. 103, 1,15: PL 37, 1348.

[28] Examples are in the *Ugaritic Keret* epic where exchange took place between King Pabil and Udm through messengers also called *Angel*; or the messenger of the Phoenician deity *Milk Astarte*, etc. The premonition of Maria Pia Giudici seems conclusive: "It should not disconcert us unduly to learn that the goddess Asherah, in the belief of the ancient Semitic peoples, had servants such as Rades and Amran who were 'reflections of the glory of their Lord' and were esteemed as "angels" by these same ancient people." (cf. M. P GIUDICI, *The Angels – Spiritual and Exegetical Notes*, tr. Edmund C. Lane, SSP, NY: Alba House, 1995, 1998, p. 13).

2.1 SOME OF THE BIBLICAL PRESUPPOSITION ON THE EXISTENCE OF ANGELS

Commonly critical minds put this question when mention is made of Angels: "how do you know that they exist?" For fear of error in answering this question many avoid venturing into *the space* of the Angels. However, if one takes the secular world as my immediate audience, it would be an uphill task to provide logical proof as is the issue of God's existence. But if the world religions are the audience, the polemics would centre more on the religious conceptions of the *form* of their existence. And when Christians are my audience, as in this case, the beautifully simplified summary given by Joan Carroll Cruz, a tertiary of Discalced Carmelite Order is a good way forward. Responding to the question, "How do you know that Angels exist?" she writes:

> *The answer can be briefly summarized in this manner: we know that angels exist from the teaching of the Church, which is based both on Sacred Scripture – the Old and the New Testaments – and on Tradition, from the unanimous teachings of the Saints and Doctors of the Church, and from the innumerable well-authenticated accounts of apparitions.*[29]

Of all the sources mentioned by Cruz, we will discuss the existence of Angels according to the Scriptures.

The Scripture has no explicit information on "how" the Angels came to exist but presupposes their creation before the foundation of the world. Psalm 148 brings the fact of their creation out; calling upon all in the celestial heavens, including the angels, to praise God. The reason given is, *"For He commanded and they were created"* (Ps. 148:1-5). The time of their creation is never stated, however, we know they were created before the creation of the world. From the book of Job we are told that they were present when the earth was created (cf. Job 38:4-7) so their creation was prior to the creation of the universe as described in Genesis chapter

---

[29] J. C., CRUZ, *Angels and Devils*, Rockford, IL: Tan Book Pub., 1999, p.4.

one.[30] The agent of their creation is specifically stated to be Christ as the One through whom all things were created (cf. John 1:1-3 with Col. 1:16). [31]

Angels are mentioned in many books of the Bible. In some of the books, they are mentioned in a vivid way that their activities are obvious. Take the instances of:

   i.   The visits of the angels to Abraham (Gn. 18), Lot (Gen. 19) and in the Letter to the Hebrews 13:2

   ii.   The appearance of the Angel to Moses (Ex. 3: 2), in Ac. 7: 30, 35; or

   iii.   The part of Angels in the giving of the Law in Ac. 7:38, 53; Gal. 3, 19 and Heb. 2, 2.

In other instances, Angels are mentioned but their mission and activities are not as explicit as above instances.[32] What I am eager to point out here is that the Scripture has good record of their existence. From NT records, some instances where Christ himself taught of their existence are worth outlining. Jesus teaches;

1. In Mt. 18, 10: *"See that you never despise any of these little ones, for I tell you that their angels in heaven are continually in the presence of my Father in heaven"*.

2. In Mt 24, 31: *"And he will send out his angels with a loud trumpet call, and they will gather his elect from the four winds, from one end of heaven to the other"*.

---

[30] Gen. 1, 1 - *"In the beginning God created heaven and earth"*: The function of the particle 'and' is to show the connection between the celestial world of the Angels and the earthly world of men. This is confirmed again in Neh 9, 6 - *"You are the LORD, you alone; you have made heaven, the heaven of heavens, with all their host, the earth and all that is on it, the seas and all that is in them. To all of them you give life, and the host of heaven worships you."*

[31] In Col. 1, 15-17 St. Paul teaches that the invisible world came to be through Christ: He is the image of the unseen God, the first-born of all creation, for in him were created all things in heaven and on earth: everything visible and everything invisible, thrones, ruling forces, sovereignties, powers -- all things were created through him and for him. The same theology St. John repeated in the power of the pre-existence of the Logos in 1, 1-3.visible and everything invisible, thrones, ruling forces, sovereignties, powers -- all things were created through him and for him. The same theology St. John repeated in the power of the pre-existence of the Logos in 1, 1-3.

[32] That various writers have different enumeration of the occurrences of the word, supports the fact that their mentioning in some instances are not obvious: For Cruz, they are mentioned in 31 of 46 book of the OT (Cf. Op. cit. p.5) and in NT 158 times (in the Gospels, Epistles and Apocalypse – Ibid. p. 8); For Fred Dickason, Angels are referred to in 34 of the 66 books of the Bible. They are mentioned 108 times in the Old Testament and 165 times in the New Testament. (Cf. C. F., DICKASON, *Angels: Elect and Evil* Chicago: Moody, 1975, p. 13); still for another author, "…these celestial beings are referred to from 294 to 305 times in the Bible. References to angels occur at least 116 times in the Old Testament and 175 times in the New Testament" (Cf., J. H., KEATHLEY *Angel, God's Ministering Spirits,* online: http://www.bible.org/page.asp?page_id=711.)

3. In Mt. 26, 53 *"Do you think that I cannot appeal to my Father, and he will at once send me more than twelve legions of angels?"*

4. In John 1:50-51, Jesus said to Nathanael, *"Do you believe because I told you that I saw you under the fig tree? You will see greater things than these... Very truly, I tell you, you will see heaven opened and the angels of God ascending and descending upon the Son of Man"*.

5. In Lk. 12:8-9: *"Whoever acknowledges me before men, the Son of Man likewise will acknowledge him before the angels of God, but whoever denies me before men will be denied before the angels of God"*

All these are obvious indications that in the Scripture as well as in the teachings of Jesus, the existence of the Angels are presupposed. Other numerous biblical texts speak in different fashions of Angels: some speak of Angels in a popular way intended to be edifying; some are used in a figurative sense to describe the grandeur or the Providence of God; but some speak of the authentic presence of angels. When, for instance Jesus said, *"Whoever acknowledges me before men, the Son of Man likewise will acknowledge him before the angels of God, but whoever denies me before men will be denied before the angels of God"*, he was surely not speaking in figurative sense. On the contrary, he cited the Angels as concrete realities for His witnesses.[33] One can understand this to mean that Angels really exist.

In other words, the Sacred Scriptures presuppose that the Angels exit. These Scriptural presuppositions have been the foundation of Christian (especially Catholic) theology on the Angels. From the Scriptures, we have the theological descriptions that give us clues about their nature. We will outline briefly some of these descriptions.

---

[33] M. P., GIUDICI, Op. cit. pp. 25-26.

2.2 SOME OF THE BIBLICAL DESCRIPTION OF THE NATURE OF THE ANGELS

We would like to use four biblical descriptions of Angels to point out their nature:

1. As *Personal* Beings
2. As *Spirit* Beings
3. As Being with more communicable *attributes* than man
4. As Beings organized and ranked in *hierarchies*.

2.2.1 Angels as Personal Beings

The Bible describes Angels as Personal Beings from the activities they perform. In the passages like 2 Sam. 14:20, Mt. 24:36, Mt. 28:5 and others,[34] one can discern three major qualities of personhood: They have intellect; they express emotions and they have the will. I will briefly explain each of these.

2.2.1.1 Angelic Intellect: (cf. Matt.28:5; 1 Pet.1:12)

Angels were created with intelligence and wisdom. This knowing faculty in the Angels helped the Angel of the resurrection who was at the tomb when the women seeking the body of Jesus arrived to redirect them to go and announce the risen Christ to the brethren and to tell them that He has gone ahead of them to Galilee where they will see Him (cf. Mt. 28:5-7). Donald Hagner comments that "It is not uncommon for such heavenly messengers similarly to exhort those whom they approach not to fear (e.g., Luke 1:13, 30; 2:10; pertaining to Jesus, 14:27; 17:7; Rev 1:17)"[35].

Angels know their future, or in the case of fallen angels, their doom. Angels know and recognize their adversaries as exemplified by fallen angels recognizing Jesus (cf. Matt. 8, 28-29; Mk 5, 2-20; Lk. 8, 26-39) and the apostle Paul (cf. Acts 19, 13-15). Fallen angels also know about the triune nature of God and their efforts to deceive men to turn away from the worship of God. And Angels have moral knowledge; they know what is morally right and wrong. However

---

[34] Good instances could be found in, Lk. 4:33-34, Mt. 8:28-29, Acts 19:15, Jm. 2:19, and 1 Tim. 4:1-3.

[35] D. A , HAGNER, *Word Biblical Commentary, Volume 33b: Matthew 14-28*, Dallas, Texas: Word Books, Publisher, 1998, p. 78.

Angels are not omniscient; they do not know all things like God (cf. Matt. 24:36) but their knowledge is more perfect than human intelligence because they are not limited by matter, space and time like man. The Angelic intelligence and knowledge is perfect because it is pure and free from material contamination in its created existence and has no essential relation with materiality in their mode of operation.

2.2.1.2 Angelic emotions: (Job 38:7; Luke 2:13; 15:10)

As personal beings, Angels are described in the Bible to manifest emotions. They rejoiced at the birth of the Messiah (Lk. 2:13); they rejoice at the return of a sinner (cf. Lk. 15:10) and are pictured as shouting "with joy" at the break of the day (cf. Job 38:7).[36]

2.2.1.3 Angelic Will: (Jude 6)

Free will is a constitutive make-up of every being with spiritual nature, whether divine, angelic or human. Angels as pure spirits must have freedom of choice which involves willing. Since the Bible says that "God did not spare the Angels that sinned"[37], sinning in Angels implies willing. Pascal Parente supports this where he writes:

Sacred Scripture clearly implies the existence of a free will in the Angelic nature. The mere fact that a number of them sinned while the rest chose to remain loyal to God proves it beyond doubt. Personal sin is a willful transgression of the law of God. Sin cannot exist where there is no free will. Since the Scripture explicitly reveals the sin of the Angels and their banishment from heaven, it clearly implies that they are in possession of a free will[38]

---

[36] From the fallen Angels too, the demons, we see the emotion of "fear" (Mk 1:23, 24; 5:7), of "shuddering" (Jm. 2:19); and of "anger" (Rev. 12:17).
[37] Cf. 2 Pet. 2:4.
[38] PARENTE, P., *The Angelic Nature and its Operations*, online article: http://www.ewtn.com/library/MARY/angel2.htm. Accessed on 18/02/2011.

Unlike human beings, angelic will is entirely free from passions and all sensitive appetites, because *their act of will* is determined exclusively by the *Angelic mind* with a decision and a firmness that is final and admits of no reverse. It is exactly this quality of the Angelic will that makes the faithful Angel pure and free from imperfections; on the other hand, makes the fallen angels incapable of conversion and repentance. Whereas the good Angel that has once elicited an act of love of God will love God for all eternity, a demon wills aversion with God and remains in eternal enmity with Him. This is exactly the subject matter of the letter of St. Jude, verse 6: "*And the angels who did not keep their own position, but left their proper dwelling, he has kept in eternal chains in deepest darkness for the judgment of the great Day.*"

2.2.1.4 Angels as Spirit Beings

According to biblical description of their nature, Angels are created by God as pure Spirits without any material body (Heb. 1:14). "Pure Spirit" means that the angelic nature is entirely spiritual, that an Angel has no body and is not dependent on material body either for its existence or its operations.[39] As Pure Spirits with immaterial body, they are superior to man but still inferior to God. Unlike God, they cannot be omnipresent. They can only be at a place at a time, although not bound by space and time (cf. Dan. 9:21-23; 10:10-14). But sometimes, by divine volition or mission, they can appear in human body.[40]

Again, as Pure Spirits created by God, the bible describes them as immortal[41] and incapable of reproduction (cf. Lk. 20:36).

2.2.2 Angels as Beings with more Communicable Attributes

Attributes in God, in a simple language, are those qualities or characteristics that form part of the very essence of who God is – the things that describe God – For e.g., God is Absolute, Self-existent, Self-sufficient, Immutable or Eternal (these are His *incommunicable Attributes* which He does not share with His creatures). But that God is Loving, Holy, Just, Compassionate,

---

[39] Cf. Online Dictionary from *New Catholic Dictionary*, http://www.catholic-forum.com/saints/ncd06795.htm. Accessed on 27/02/2006.
[40] In dreams – Matt.1:20; in natural sight with human functions – Gen.18:1-8, 22; 19:1; seen by some and not others – 2 Kings 6:15-17.
[41] Cf. Mk 12, 25

Wise, Truth, etc (these are His *communicable Attributes* which He shares with the Angels and man). But Angels' attributes are more or higher than man's because of their immaterial nature. Some of the biblical descriptions of Angels show Angels as Beings with more communicable attributes than man. The Angelic attributes are higher than human attributes but lower than God's.[42] These attributes further helps us to understand their nature as superior to man.

The interesting thing in these Scriptural revelations about the Angels is that in spite of their sublime nature, in spite of their superiority to man, God has put them in the service of man. This is what marveled our Patriarch David in Psalm 8:3-5 when he questioned such an honour to man:

> *When I look at your heavens, the work of your fingers, the moon and the stars that you have established;[4] what are human beings that you are mindful of them, mortals that you care for them[5] Yet you have made them a little lower than God, and crowned them with glory and honour. [6] You have given them dominion over the works of your hands; you have put all things under their feet...[43]*

Later on, in Psalm 91:11, while he prayed for protection in the Temple, David relies in the promises of God to put him (David) under the care/charge of His holy Angels who guards him in all his ways! God makes His Angels to serve man!

2.2.3   Angels as Beings Organized in Ranks

The last Scriptural description of the nature of the Angels we would like to discuss is that Angels are ranked in a hierarchical order. To discuss the ranks of Angels according to the Scriptures, it is important to note that while the Scripture revealed all the Angels in their different orders or ranks, the classification or ranking as we have it today is not according to the

---

[42] For instance, they have more knowledge than man (Mtt.24, 31; Lk 1, 13-16) but less than God (Mtt.24, 36). They have more power than man (2 Pet.2, 11; Acts 5, 19) but less than God.

[43] Some translations like King James' Version (KJV) translates verse 5: "*For thou hast made him a little lower than the angels, and hast crowned him with glory and honour...*" For such God-fearing men of old like David, it is really a marvel what God has done in creation, how much honour He bestowed to man.

Scriptures.[44] Much of what we have is a theological development along the ages. This is the findings of a researcher in angelology,

> We obtain our information about certain ranks of the heavenly army from hints given us in the Scripture. In the Old Testament books of Exodus and Isaias we are introduced to the Seraphim and Cherubim. In the New Testament we learn of Angels and Archangels. The remaining choirs are given us by St. Paul, who wrote that all things were created by God in Heaven and on earth... "thrones or dominations, or principalities, or powers..." (Col. 1:16). And again, "Above all principality, and power, and virtue, and dominion, and every name that is named." These, plus other statements in Scripture, firmly established the existence of nine choirs of angels as early as the time of St. Ignatius the Martyr (d. 107), who mentions the hierarchies and the ranks of angels in his Epistle to the Trallians: "I am in chains and able to grasp heavenly things, the ranks of the Angels, the hierarchy of principalities, things visible and invisible" [45]

To conclude this part of our exposition on the nature of the Angels, we have noted that the Angels from the Scripture have the nature of personal beings; of Spirit Beings; with communicable attributes and are organized in ranks. My effort in this part is only to indicate that the Scripture said something with regards to the nature of Angels. The reader needs further reading through good Theological books like the *Summa Theologica* of St. Thomas Aquinas to get in-depth knowledge on this.[46]

In the last part of this chapter, we will make effort to give a simple co-ordination between the Scriptural basis and the Catholic tradition on the classification of the Angels before we settle on the central point of our attention – the ministry of the Angels.

---

[44] G. HERRICK, *Angelology: Angels,* On line article: Cf. http://www.bible.org/page.asp?page_id=729. 20/07/2007.

[45] J. C., CRUZ, *Angels and Devils,* Rockford, IL: Tan Book Pub., 1999, p.94.

[46] Cf. Summa Theologica, Prima Part (I), especially from number 108.

2.3 ON THE HIERARCHY OF THE ANGELS: A BRIEF HISTORICAL OVERVIEW

The root origin of angelic hierarchy, as we have described above, is the Scriptures. But the organizational order of this hierarchy does not originate from the Scriptures.[47] Hence, it would not be proper to make use of this order without indicating its source and development along the ages, at least in a compact manner.

Records of studies and contacts with the Angels go back throughout history. Peter B. Lloyd in his online essay noted that contact with disembodied beings is not new. In fact, reports of such contact go back throughout history: they occur in the Scriptures and other venerated texts and accounts of them are found in both the formal religious doctrines and in folklores. Throughout the Middle Eastern and European religious traditions, they have been known as *'Angels'*.[48]

One can recognize the truth in what Peter Lloyd said because people's religious experience, are highly influenced by what they received by transmission (from the Scripture, other sacred texts and traditions) and what they receive are precedent-records of their ancestors' religious faith-experience. The Bible and other traditional records formed the earliest source of Catholic angelology.[49] Lloyd citing Connolly pointed out one major source of organizing angelic hierarchy as the sixth-century text: *The Celestial Hierarchy and Mystical Theology*. This text were used first in the Eastern Churches as foundational to Christian study on arrangement and grouping of Angels till later the translation from Greek made it available to the Western Church as well.[50] This text is attributed to Dionysius the Areopagite.

---

[47] "*The Bible has no systematic ordering of angels. Even in the book of Revelation their range cannot be analyzed with any precision*". Cf. J., LANG, *The Angels of God: Understanding the Bible*, London, New City Press, 1997, p. 74.

[48] P.B., LLOYD, *Angels in Religious Traditions*, Online article: http://easyweb.easynet.co.uk/~ursa/angels/trad.htm. Accessed on 18 / 03/2006.

[49] Peter Lloyd traced the earliest sources to David Conolly's book 'In Search of the Angels' cited in his article: "*The pan-religious scope of the tradition is indicated by Connolly: The particular western notion of benevolent spirit beings that most people today would quickly identify as angels developed from Judeo-Christian and Islamic lore, which were in turn influenced by earlier Persian, Greek, Babylonian, Chaldean, and Sumerian beliefs, among others...*"

[50] Loc. cit.

Dionysius the Areopagite had been converted to Christianity by St. Paul[51], and later became a bishop in 1st century Athens. It was believed that St. Paul taught Dionysius revealed knowledge about the angels, which he (Paul) in turn received from the Lord. For this reason any work by Dionysius enjoyed apostolic authority.[52] This text, *Celestial Hierarchy*, was later endorsed by Pope Gregory the Great (c. 590 to 604 AD) and in the medieval ages were accepted by St. Thomas Aquinas who used it as a foundation for his angelology.

However, the later discovery that this text attributed to Dionysius was probably written by a Syrian monk of late 5th or early 6th century, gave it the name *Pseudo* Dionysius. That notwithstanding, the text remained the main source from which great teachers of the Catholic faith like Gregory the great, Aquinas and others relied for their angelology. In fact, the table below gives the traditional picture of Patristic Angelic hierarchies which have remained foundational to present day additions, subtractions or rearrangements:[53]

Ambrose	Gregory the Great	John of Damascus	Pseudo-Dionysius
1. Seraphim	1. Seraphim	1. Seraphim	Triadic 1a. Seraphim
2. Cherubim	2. Cherubim	2. Cherubim	1b. Cherubim
3. Powers	3.Thrones	3.Thrones	1c. Thrones
4. Dominions	4. Dominions	4. Dominions	Triadic 2a. Dominions
5. Thrones	5.Principalities	5. Powers	2b. Powers
6. Archangels	6. Powers	6. Authorities	2c. Authorities
7. Angels	7. Virtues	7. Rulers	Triadic 3a. Principalities
	8. Archangels	8. Archangels	3b. Archangels
	9. Angels	9. Angels	3c. Angels

---

[51] Acts 17:34 - "*But some of them joined him and became believers, including Dionysius the Areopagite and a woman named Damaris, and others with them.*"

[52] P.B., LLOYD, Loc. cit.: He writes "This supposition was seemingly corroborated by the writings themselves asserting that the author had been taught in part by Hierotheus, a pupil of Paul's, and by Paul himself. Therefore any writings believed to be by Dionysius were revered and held in almost as high a regard as the Bible itself." (cf. P.B., LLOYD, Loc. cit.).

[53] Like Billy Graham, a contemporary American Preacher would prefer his own list begin with the Archangels at the topmost and run thus: 1. Archangels 2. Angels 3.Seraphim 4.Cherubim 5.Principalities 6.Authorities 7.Powers 8.Thrones 9.Might. Cf. Online:
http://www.hymnsandcarolsofchristmas.com/Angels/heirarchy.htm. Accessed on 18 / 03/2007.

In summary, from the patristic times, Catholic tradition has classified Angels in between seven and nine *ranks* or *choirs*. However, as the chart above demonstrates, there is little unanimity in the details. For our exposition, the triadic distinction in the Pseudo-Dionysius will help much in illustrating the ministry of the ranks as we would see in the next segment. Thus, we will be adopting the Pseudo-Dionysian hierarchy.

CHAPTER THREE:

HE WILL PUT YOU IN HIS ANGELS' CHARGE (Ps. 91:11-13)

3.1   Ministry of the Angels in the Context of Psalm 91.

In this section, we would be a little bit technical with the biblical facts presented in the context of Psalm 91. I crave the reader's indulgence with these technicalities if they are boring because they are necessary to background a good understanding of the charge God has given His Angels over us.

In the entire Psalter, Psalm 91 lacks an original title[54] and the time of its composition could not be easily determined.[55] One needs to place back Psalm 91 in its original context in order to understand and appreciate its message. Biblical scholars have not agreed much in replacing the original context of this Psalm. The Biblical Scribes (Hagiographers) contextually places Psalms 90-100 among the "Moses-Collection" because these Psalms were "designed to call the Israelite communities and individuals who returned from the exile to a wise and confident faith in the kingship of Yahweh, and to set forth that 'Yahweh is the Great God / and the Great King over all gods' (95:3)"[56]

The Psalmist in 90:17 prays for the salvation of His '*People*', asking Yahweh to reveal His favour on His *People* and to prosper their handiwork.[57] Then, in Psalm 91 Yahweh responds to this prayer with many promises, concluding with: "*I will satisfy them with long life and show them my salvation*". Here the work of Yahweh is realized, i.e. salvation for His people.[58] Also, in Ps. 90:1, God is a "dwelling place" which is re-echoed in Ps.91:9. This 'dwelling place' in 91:9

---

[54] It was inscribed by the LXX without any warrant (title) '*to David*'. Cf. F., DELITZSCH, et al. (eds), *Commentary on the Old Testament in Ten Volumes*, vol. v, transl. James Martin, Grand Rapids, Michigan: William Eerdmans Pub., 19.., p.61.

[55] Derek Kidner concludes that "... it is in infact anonymous and timeless, perhaps all the more accessible for that." Cf. D., KIDNER, *Psalm 73-150 a Commentary on Books III-V of the Psalms*, Leicester, England: Inter-Varsity Press, 1973, p.331.

[56] T.E., MARVIN, *The World Biblical Commentary (WBC), Volume 20: Psalms 51-100*, Dallas, Texas: Word Books, Publisher, 1998, p.452.

[57] Ps. 90, 17 – "*Let the favor of the Lord our God be upon us, and prosper for us the work of our hands - O prosper the work of our hands!*"

[58] F., DELITZSCH, et al. (eds), Op. cit. p.61.

is again linked to the next Psalm (92:11) with description of God as "the Most High"; and His people described as looking triumphantly upon their foes (Compare Pss. 91:8 and 92:11). All these center on the divine response to the anguished prayer of those whose trust in Him.[59]

Many modern biblical scholars have commented on the attempt to recover the original context of Psalm 91 – that is, who the Psalm addressed originally? Some commentators[60] have supposed that the psalm should be understood as addressed to a king. J. Eaton says, "The individual on whom such promises are lavished could hardly be any but the king". In this sense, the psalm climaxes a liturgical worship service in which a Priest or a Prophet encourages a King to meet the threat of an enemy and "set out for the scene of battle with the confident assurance that under Yahweh's protection he will emerge both unscathed and victorious".[61] Mowinckel,[62] further combines the idea of *protection* with fear against demonic attacks as the proper context of the Psalm. For him, the psalm has the form of a liturgy, spoken by a priest in response to a worshiper who has come to a worship place to pray to Yahweh for *deliverance* from life-threatening conditions. Schmidt[63] takes the psalm as a form of "entrance liturgy" similar to Ps 121, addressed to *pilgrims* coming to the temple. Delekat[64] argues that psalm 91 is a priestly speech to someone who seeks *protection for himself and for his family* in the sanctuary from the onslaught of a pestilence.

As a present-day reader, I see the context of Psalm 91 as combining the opinions of all the commentators if it is read within the liturgical worship of a present day pious Christian. As baptized Christians, a present-day worshipper, shares through his baptism in the triple roles of being a king, a prophet and a priest in the body of Christ (the church or the worshipping community). Thus, J. Eaton's comment is right. In their liturgical worship and prayers, Christ teaches his disciples to say the Lord's Prayer asking God for protection and deliverance from all evil (forces). Hence, Mowinckel's comment is also right. Every Christian is a pilgrim on the

---

[59] R.J., CLIFFORD, *Abingdon Old Testament Commentaries (AOTC)* Psalm 73-150, Nashville: Abingdon Press, 2003, p.102.

[60] J. H., EATON, *Kingship and the Psalms.* SBT 2.32. London: SCM Press, 1976, p.17

[61] A. R., JOHNSON, *The Cultic Prophet and Israel's Psalmody.* Cardiff: University of Wales Press, 1979, p.188. (cf. Caquot, *Sem.* [1958] 21–37; Dahood, II, 329). (*Psalmenstudien,*)

[62] S., MOWINCKEL, *Psalmenstudien.* III, in *WBC* Oslo: Kristiana, 1921–24.62. pp. 102–5.

[63] Comparing Pss 15 and 24A, Cf. H., SCHMIDT, *Die Psalmen.* HAT 15. in *WBC* Tübingen: Mohr (Siebeck), 1934.63, pp.171–73

[64] L., DELEKAT *Asylie und Schutzorakel am Zionheiligtum: Eine Untersuchung zur den privaten Feindpsalmen,* in *WBC* Leiden: Brill, 1967.64, pp.235–39.

journey to our eternal home. Schmidt is therefore right. Delekat is very right if we consider that Christians have been taught by Jesus Christ to ask the Father for anything in His name. So asking for personal protection or family protection against all kinds of pestilence is not out of liturgical context.

Therefore, I am reading Psalm 91 as having the setting of a liturgical context for today's pious Christian who, as a believer, worships within a community of the 'returning-new-Israelites',[65] i.e., those who take shelter under the shadow of the Most High and says to Yahweh from the sincerity of their hearts; "LORD, YOU ARE MY GOD, MY REFUGE IN WHOM I TRUST!" I am sure God responds to such Christians with the entire promises in Psalm 91:

[3] *... He will deliver you from the snare of the fowler and from the deadly pestilence;*

[4] *He will cover you with his pinions, and under his wings you will find refuge;*

His faithfulness is a shield and buckler.

[5] *You will not fear the terror of the night, or the arrow that flies by day,*

[6] *or the pestilence that stalks in darkness, or the destruction that wastes at noonday.*

[7] *A thousand may fall at your side, ten thousand at your right hand, but it will not come near you.*

[8] *You will only look with your eyes and see the punishment of the wicked.*

[9] *Because you have made the LORD your refuge, the Most High your dwelling place,*

[10] *no evil shall befall you, no scourge come near your tent.*

[11] **For He will command His angels concerning you to guard you in all your ways.**

---

[65] I do not mean by this phrase a supersession of the Israelites of old but a universalizing of the old Israel beyond the territorial confines of Hebrew People to contain all who returns to the acknowledgement of Yahweh as One and Only God, submitting to His Lordship and asking for His protection and provision.

¹² On their hands they will bear you up, so that you will not dash your foot against a stone.

¹³ You will tread on the lion and the adder, the young lion and the serpent you will trample under foot.

¹⁴ *Those who love me, I will deliver; I will protect those who know my name.*

¹⁵ *When they call to me, I will answer them; I will be with them in trouble, I will rescue them and honor them.*

¹⁶ *With long life I will satisfy them, and show them my salvation.*

Having placed the entire Psalm 91 within a context, we limit our attention to verses 11-13 marked above in bold. These verses are the centre of our discussion on the ministry of the Holy Angels. These verses help us to understand the extent God the Almighty is willing to assist man.

3.2 DELIMITING THE CONTEXT OF PSALM 91 TO THE MINISTRY OF ANGELS

Psalm 91 has 16 verses. It is divided into two major parts, accepted by majority of biblical scholars: vv 1-13 and vv 14-16. The first part (1-13) form a *sermonette* of encouragement while the latter part (14-16) consists of a *divine oracle* with God assumed as the speaker.[66] The entire Psalm, from the literary style, contains three fold promises of assistance which progressively decrease in length: verses 1-8; verses 9-13; and verses 14-16.[67]

The ministry of Angels falls within the first two promises (first major part – the *sermonette*). Within this part, from the structure of the verses, we can identify three other basic units that form a whole – a *pericope*.

On the whole, the first part form a twofold structural division with a distinct progression, pictured by a commentator thus:[68]

---

[66] E., MARVIN, *Psalms 51-100* in *WBC., Vol. 20* Dallas, Texas: Word Books, Publisher, 1998, p.450.

[67] R.J., CLIFFORD, *Abingdon Old Testament Commentaries* (AOTC), Op. cit. p.102.

[68] F. E., GAEBELEN, et al, (eds), *The Expositor's Bible Commentary*, vol. 5, Grand Rapids: Zondervan Pub. House, 1991, p.598.

A.	Invitation to the Protection of God (vv 1-2)

    B.	Forms of Protection (vv 3-8)

A*	Invitation to the Protection of God (vv 9-10)

    B*	Forms of Protection (vv 11- 13)

C	The Oracle of Salvation (vv 14-16)

Looking at the above structure, there are two *invitations* (A and A*) and two responses in forms of protection (B and B*). The first invitation in A (vv1-2), made in an impersonal third person, is to all who seek God as their highest good, what in sapiential literature is called *wisdom*.[69] But the second invitation in A* (vv 9-10) made to "*You*"[70] who has chosen God as a refuge and the Most High as the dwelling, is responded to with promise of God to commission His Angels to minister protection unto you. Notice that in response to the first invitation (B), God's protection is presented in a metaphoric sense as a mother eagle carrying its threatened chicks to safety. But in the second invitation (B*) God sends His angels to lead the frightened individual through the perils of life.[71]

Thus, for those who seek godliness and make Yahweh their base, we notice a peculiar development in the promises given to them in vv 11-13. The negative threats in v 10 ("no harm…, no disaster…") are now complimented in a positive declaration that "he will command his angels… to guard you"[72] I am making this unit of positive promise my *locus standi* (starting point) in presenting a biblical interpretation of the ministry of the Angels.

Many Christians out there have with all their heart submitted to the Lordship of Jesus Christ and have accepted Him as the Master and Lord of their lives. They have also in principles taken the Word of God as the main source of their spiritual life. Yet, they know little of the charge God has given to these benevolent heavenly ministers (the Angels) over their lives. They practically make little or no use of the riches God have lavishly provided for them through the assistance of these heavenly friends. I wish now to attempt a presentation of these heavenly hosts

---

[69] loc. cit.

[70] V. 9 specifically states: "…because *you* have made the Lord your refuge…"

[71] Both metaphors come from the exodus tradition: the protective eagle in Exod. 19, 4 and Deut, 32, 10-12 and the guardian angel in Exod. 23, 20, 23 and 32, 34. Cf. R.J., CLIFFORD, *AOTC*, Op. cit. p.102.

[72] Compare similar charges in Ps. 34, 7; Mt. 4, 6; Lk. 4, 10-11; Heb. 1, 4.

in order of their hierarchies and ranks with the intention of proposing to every Christian more attention of honour to them and imploration of their assistance.

First, we present the Angels in their triadic hierarchy to show how they are grouped according to their area of ministration. Secondly, we present the ranks one by one beginning from the closest to the throne of God to the Guardian Angels who are closest to human beings. It will be nice to acknowledge, *ab initio*, that the presentation of the hierarchy of the Angels in this part of the work depends heavily on the Scriptures as we have back-grounded above and on the writings of the great theologians of the Church, especially that of Psuedo-Dionysius and St. Thomas Aquinas.

3.3   THE TRIADIC DIVISION AMONG THE ANGELS

With regard to the ordering of the Angels according to their functions and closeness to God, no one is obliged in faith.[73] Right from the Patristic period, attempts have been made by the doctors of the Church to interpret the Scriptural information we have on the ordering of the Angels.[74] The traditional Catholic theology on the hierarchies and ranks of the Angels is based on the hierarchical ordering of the Scholastics who were influenced by the work of Pseudo-Dionysius – its influence had been obvious:

> *The treatise "De Coelesti Hierarchia", which is ascribed to St Denis the Areopagite and which exercised so strong an influence upon the Scholastics, treats at great length of the hierarchies and orders of the angels.*[75]

Based on the same Psuedo-Dionysian work on the nine ranks or choirs of the Angels, we present St. Thomas Aquinas' contribution in grouping the nine choirs in triadic hierarchies. The importance of Aquinas' contribution to our understanding of the nine choirs is that St. Thomas

---

[73] Catholic Encylopedia: CD ROM, Windows Mac Unix, 1914 edition, s.v. *Angels*. It writes: "Though the doctrine it contains regarding the choirs of angels has been received in the Church with extraordinary unanimity, no proposition touching the angelic hierarchies is binding on our faith."

[74] Cf. Ignatius the Martyr (d. 107) on the *Epistle to the Trallians 5*; St. Gregory the Great on *Hom 34 in Evang.*; Aquinas in the *Summa Theologica* (S. Th.), I, 108; etc.

[75] Catholic Encyclopedia, ibid.

helps us to know that each of the choir belongs to a particular hierarchy because of the nature of their ministry.

St. Thomas,[76] following St. Denis[77], divides the angels into three hierarchies each of which contains three orders. Their proximity to the Supreme Being serves as the basis of this division. In the first hierarchy he places the Seraphim, Cherubim, and Thrones; in the second, the Dominations, Virtues, and Powers; in the third, the Principalities, Archangels, and Angels. St. Thomas offered a lucid explanation with regards to this Triadic ordering. His explanation is so complete that an attempt to paraphrase would mutilate it:

> *Let us then first examine the reason for the ordering of Dionysius, in which we see, that, as said above (1), the highest hierarchy contemplates the ideas of things in God Himself; the second in the universal causes; and third in their application to particular effects. And because God is the end not only of the angelic ministrations, but also of the whole creation, it belongs to the first hierarchy to consider the end; to the middle one belongs the universal disposition of what is to be done; and to the last belongs the application of this disposition to the effect, which is the carrying out of the work; for it is clear that these three things exist in every kind of operation. So Dionysius, considering the properties of the orders as derived from their names, places in the first hierarchy those orders the names of which are taken from their relation to God, the "Seraphim," "Cherubim," and "Thrones"; and he places in the middle hierarchy those orders whose names denote a certain kind of common government or disposition--the "Dominations," "Virtues," and "Powers"; and he places in the third hierarchy the orders whose names denote the execution of the work, the "Principalities," "Angels," and "Archangels."[78]*

St. Thomas gave three main reasons above as the basis of the triadic ordering. Putting them in a simple way to make it easily graspable;

---

[76] *S. Th.* I, 108.
[77] *De Coelesti Hierarchia*, vi, vii
[78] S. Th. I, 108.

1. First, St. Thomas finds the main reason to group the Dionysian ranks in three in the ways these Holy Beings focus (or as he used it – *"contemplates the idea of..."*) their ministerial attention: The first group focuses on *God Himself*; the second on the *Universal Causes* and the third on the *Application of the universal to particular effects.*

2. Secondly, he finds in the Dionysian ordering that the Angelic ministry is ultimately directed to one end – God, the first group *directly serves God*, the second directly oversees *Universal disposition to serve God*, while the third puts to the *Universal disposition to serve God to practical effect.*

3. Thirdly, from above two reasons then, St. Thomas said he noticed that Dionysius puts in the first group – *Seraphim, Cherubim* and *Thrones* – those Angels whose name indicate closeness to God; then in the second group – *Dominations, Virtues* and *Powers* – because their names indicate universal government or disposition, and finally in the last group those Angels whose name imply practical execution of work – *Principalities, Angels* and *Archangels.*

Surely, many would immediately react on finding the Archangels on the last rung of the ladder. Let us take each of the triad as a group to understand better why St. Thomas and traditional Catholic theology prefers this ordering.

3.3.1   The First Triad: *Seraphim, Cherubim and Thrones*

To bring out what '*contemplating God in Himself*' means among the triadic group is best seen in the ministry they perform. With regard to their ministry, the first triad considers the end or goal of all ministration which is God. Interpreting this in simple language, Cruz writes,

> *Tradition, as well as the opinions of theologians and the Doctors of the Church, agree that these three choirs (Seraphim, Cherubim and Thrones)[79] are closest to*

---

[79] Bracket mine.

the throne of God and are occupied with adoration and with singing the praises of God. [80]

Thus, in consideration of the end for which the Angels and the entire creation were made by God, the first triad, who are closest to the sublime divinity of God, live only to adore him. Indeed, the entire creation is made to adore God, but this triad is specifically made with the disposition of adoring God unceasingly as creatures closest to him. St. Thomas pictures that there are some who enjoy the dignity of being able with familiarity to approach the king or leader; others in addition are privileged to know his secrets; and others above these ever abide with him, in a close union. According to this similitude, we can understand the disposition in the orders of the first hierarchy; for the "Thrones" are raised up so as to be the familiar recipients of God in themselves, in the sense of knowing immediately the types of things in Himself; and this is proper to the whole of the first hierarchy. Consequently, "the 'Cherubim' know the Divine secrets super-eminently; and the 'Seraphim' excel in what is the supreme excellence of all, in being united to God Himself; and all this in such a manner that the whole of this hierarchy can be called the 'Thrones'; as, from what is common to all the heavenly spirits together, they are all called 'Angels.'"[81]

In summary, it belongs to the first triad to praise and adore God. This constitutes the end of their ministry: to worship God. The nature and manner of their worship is akin to the way they know and receive from God. This is what St. Thomas means when he says that the *Thrones* are raised to be familiar recipients of God and they know God in themselves; the *Cherubim* on the other hand know God super-eminently; while the *Seraphim* "excel in what is the supreme excellence of all".[82] From this one can notice that the stratification within the Triad itself is according to the mode with which they receive from the divinity of God. We shall see this clearly when we take each of the rank individually.

---

[80] J. C., CRUZ, *Angels and Devils*, Rockford, IL: Tan Book Pub., 1999, p. 97.
[81] S. Th., Loc. cit.
[82] Loc. cit.

3.3.2 The Second Triad: *Dominations, Virtues and Powers*

As the first triad is committed to the end or goal of Angelic ministration – which is praising God, the second triad is committed to the universal disposition to the same divine praise. Since in their being, they contemplate the idea of things in universal causes, their ministry is centered with the governance of the universe. They have in themselves all that is required for this according to St. Thomas,

> *As regards government, three things are comprised therein, the first of which is to appoint those things which are to be done, and this belongs to the "Dominations"; the second is to give the power of carrying out what is to be done, which belongs to the "Virtues"; the third is to order how what has been commanded or decided to be done can be carried out by others, which belongs to the "Powers."*[83]

One could notice that apart from their relatedness to God, the names of the ranks in these triads denote their mission. "Dominations" for instance have to do with the authority of appointing tasks for the governance of the universe. For this they could also be called "Rulers" or "Dominions". [84] The supreme message of Paul to the Ephesians in 1, 20-22 was that Christ, having been raised and seated at God's right hand, now takes universal dominion of all the ruling powers. A commentator writes that it was this conception that underlies "…the universality of Christ's rule over any imaginable cosmic forces and brings home to believers that they have no possible justification for considering themselves under the control of such powers.[85] This statement clearly points out that there exists ruling forces, though fallen ones[86], whose power controls the universe.

Thus, in this triad, the sum of their ministry is that while the *Dominations* appoint task; the *Virtues* empower for the accomplishment of the task and the *Powers* order how the task are performed in the governing of the universe.

---

[83] S. Th., loc. cit.
[84] Cf. Eph. 1:21; 6:12
[85] A. T., LINCOLN, *Word Biblical Commentary, Volume 42: Ephesians*, Dallas, TX: Word Books, Publisher, 1998, p. 79
[86] The fallen Angels that dominate the universal forces of which Paul says we fight to conquer with the help of Christ's dominion. Cf. Eph. 6, 10ff.

3.3.3 The Third Triad: *The Principalities, Angels and Archangels*

The last triad, as their name denotes also are those who minister to man. In their relationship with God, they are as other ranks of the Angels, still close to God because as holy Angels their subjection to God is still greater than their presiding over inferior things. But some people object to this fact and think that since this triad minister to man, they are lower than the others in the hierarchy. The Angelic Doctor (St. Thomas), in his reply to such objection explained,

> *Knowledge takes place accordingly as the thing known is in the knower; but love as the lover is united to the object loved. Now higher things are in a nobler way in themselves than in lower things; whereas lower things are in higher things in a nobler way than they are in themselves. Therefore to know lower things is better than to love them; and to love the higher things, God above all, is better than to know them.[87]*

Simply put, the Angels of this triad, like others, are in themselves still in continuous union of love to the higher Being – God. This makes them ever noble. Yet, out of the knowledge of their service for love of God, they know the lower being – man. This knowledge does not diminish their nobility but rather brings man to a higher status in relation to their service. Their service consists in announcing and executing divine things as willed for man.

Thus, the *Principalities* are initiators or beginner of divine will for man; *Angels* are actual executors of divine will in action; and the *Archangels* are special mediators or Angels of special duties in execution of the duties.[88]

---

[87] S. Th. 1, 108, Repl. Obj. 3.

[88] In S. Th., 1, 108, St. Thomas writes: "The execution of the angelic ministrations consists in announcing Divine things. Now in the execution of any action there are beginners and leaders; as in singing, the precentors; and in war, generals and officers; this belongs to the "Principalities." There are others who simply execute what is to be done; and these are the "Angels." Others hold a middle place; and these are the "Archangels," as above explained."

4. CHAPTER FOUR

THE DIVINE COMMAND TO ANGELS TO MINISTER TO MAN

4.1 UNDERSTANDING THE DIVINE "COMMAND" TO THE ANGELS IN PS. 9:11-13

The reader might find the content of this sub-title a little cumbersome to read but I deem it important to provide simple exegetical explanation on the key word "to command" in Ps. 9:11 in order to demonstrate the actual nature of the charge God has given the Angels *concerning* man – their ministry to man. It is important for the reader to appreciate the difficulty created in the different translations and usage of preferred vocabularies or synonyms of the same word in the English versions of the Bible.

Here, at the centre of our text in verse 11, according to the translation of the New Revised Standard Version (*NRSV*) [89] we read: *For He will command his angels concerning you to guard you in all your ways.* The word we consider central here is the verb *ṣāwâ* (צִוָּה) - "to lay charge", "to give charge", "to command" or "to order". In our text, this verb appeared in the *Piel* form. In Hebrew language, the Piel, Pual and Hitpael have their grammatical peculiarity. As a general principle in Hebrew verbal syntax, verbs that appear in *Piel*, *Pual* or *Hitpael*, express actions in their intensive form as derived verbs. For example, while the verb *qadosh* (קָדַשׁ) in the Qal form means "to be holy", in the Piel form it means "to sanctify". The Piel form always expresses the active aspect of the intensive action of the verb. This basic knowledge would help us to understand our text within its proper usage and context. [90]

One would like the reader to see other places that the same verb '*to command*' (*ṣāwâ*) appeared in the OT accounts, especially in the historical books in order to mark the significant changes in meaning a particular translation can give the word. In Genesis 2: 16, the divine *command* to Adam not to eat of the fruit of the tree of knowledge of good and evil appeared in a waw-consecutive apocopate Piel: "*wayücaw yhwh('ädönäy) 'élöhîm `al-hä| 'ädämô*" – "Then

---

[89] The NRSV has been our preferred version in this work. Using transliteration in the Bible Works, 6.0 s.v. Ps. 91:11, it reads: "Kî mal'äkäyw yücawwê-lläk lišmorkä Bükol-Düräkêkä" - (מַלְאָכָיו יְצַוֶּה־לָּךְ לִשְׁמָרְךָ בְּכָל־דְּרָכֶיךָ).

[90] DEIANA G., SPREAFICO A., A Guide to Biblical Hebrew, Roma: Urbaniana University Press, 1998, pp. 77-78.

Yahweh God laid *upon the man* this command…". In this instance, the direct object of the command, man is introduced by the preposition '*upon*' (*'al-hä| 'ädämô*). Here the sense of the verb "command" (*ṣāwâ*) is a charge given directly *upon* a person by God.

In similar way, we find in Exodus 1:22 that the *command* Pharaoh gave to his armies to kill every male has its sense determined by the prefix לְ: – "Then Pharaoh gave a command *to all his people*…". Here a charge is given by Pharaoh *to the people*. The tense and mood of the Piel form is the same with Gen. 2:16 except that the former is singular while the latter is plural but the responsibility of the charge is borne by the object of the command directly. Further examinations with Exodus 16:34; 1 Kgs 11:10[91] and Nehemaiah 7:2[92] corroborate the same point. In all the preceding texts, the last (Neh. 7:2), came closest to the sense of our text because the recipient of the command has a responsibility of the charge *over* others. Nehemaiah appointed administrators with a *charge over* others. Yet it is not completely the same with the יְצַוֶּה־לָּךְ (yücawwè-lläk) of Psalm 91, 11.

This verb *ṣāwâ* as used in Psalm 91, 11: yücawwè-lläk – יְצַוֶּה־לָּךְ (literally: *and will command to you*) unlike the above examples (with prefixes), has a suffix of 2nd person feminine singular. First of all, it seems that this grammatical construction of using a verbal suffix by the hagiographer is preferred to a pronominal suffix mostly because with the help of the *maqqeph*, the tone is shifted from the ultima word as a rule.[93] Then secondly, the prepositional sense of the command could be misunderstood if used as a prefix because '*al* (עַל) could easily be translated either like Gen 2, 16 (*upon* the man) or Neh 7, 2 (*over* others) above and in both cases the sense would be lost. But the verbal suffix better brings out that the *command* is to give *someone* charge[94] "*concerning*" another.[95] The sense that God gives his messengers (*elohim ma'alakim*) charge *concerning* (the emphasized "*you*") seems the most accurate translation of our text.

---

[91] In these citations, the prepositional prefix אֶל gives the command the sense of a charge laid "unto" the object (the person).

[92] Nehemiah give charge to administrators in the sense of "appointing over" determined by the preposition עַל translated "over".

[93] It also applies to cases like לְבָהְזָא Num 22, 6; לְקָחָה־זֹאת. Gn 2, 23; and even with ReÖsë, מֵעֲנֵה־רַךְ Pr 15, 1; וּמִשְׁנֶה־בֶּסֶף Gn 43, 15. In all these examples the tone, were it not for the *maqqeph*, would be on the ultima of the first word.

[94] Cf. BDB, Op. Cit. p.846.

[95] In most instances, the preposition 'al (עַל) introduces it. Note that this preposition is significantly different from prefix.

Other OT usages of the verb צָוָה (ṣāwâ) in the sense of giving *command concerning* others strengthen this argument further: Pharoah gave his men *command concerning* [96]Abram and they escorted him on his way with the entire house hold. The Levites performed the rites as the Lord has *commanded* Moses *concerning*[97] the Levites. The same with the woman of Tekoa whom David told: "Go to your house, I will give *order concerning*[98] you". In all these and other instances[99], the verb appeared in Piel (with occasional variation of prepositions) and bears this sense of a *command concerning* someone. Thus, the NRSV translation of the verse: "*For He will command his angels concerning you to guard you in all your ways*" renders the accurate sense of the text.

Therefore, Ps. 91:11 forms the basic platform for us to find out from the Scriptures briefly first of all, why God gave this charge to the Angels concerning man. Secondly, what *specific commands* or *charges* do the Angels have from God concerning man? These will give us ample ground to take the ranks one by one to illustrate their ministry to man.

4.2   Understanding Why God Charged the Angels Concerning Man

The Angels were originally created servants in the Divine plan of salvation: Psalm 103:20f says,

> *Bless the LORD, O you his angels, you mighty ones who do his*
> *bidding, obedient to his spoken word. Bless the LORD, all his hosts,*
> *his ministers that do his will*

Recalling the message of Psalm 91 as we stated above, there is concrete promise by God to put all who trust in him in his Angel's charge to help them overcome all obstacles on their way to salvation. This has been part of the mystery of divine plan for human salvation. St. Paul writes in Col. 1, 26: "the mystery that has been hidden throughout the ages and generations but

---

[96] Gen 12, 20
[97] Num 8, 22
[98] 2 Sam 14, 8

[99] 2 Sam. 18:5; Is 45:12, 10:6; Jer. 7:22, 39:11, Na 1:14; prefixed with ל Nu 9:8 32:38, La 1:17 Est 3:2; prefixed with אל Is 23:11 Jer. 47:7.

has now been revealed to his saints". Even Satan knows this plan very well that he reminded Jesus in their encounter in the desert saying,

> *"If you are the Son of God, throw yourself down; for it is written, 'He will command his angels concerning you,' and 'On their hands they will bear you up, so that you will not dash your foot against a stone.'"*[100]

In the OT, when Yahweh promised to lead the people of Israel to the Promised Land and the people turned aside to worship the golden calf, in faithfulness to his promise, Yahweh told Moses, *"But now go, lead the people to the place about which I have spoken to you; see, my angel shall go in front of you. Nevertheless, when the day comes for punishment, I will punish them for their sin."*[101] The identity of the divine messengers (Angels) is coterminous with their office of serving God and bringing man to his divine destination – salvation.

> *In the New Testament angels are described as 'ministering spirits, sent forth to serve [eis diakononian lit. 'into service'] (Heb. 1:14). This term has particular application to the angelic ministry, not only because of its use as a form of ecclesiastical service, that of a deacon, but for an earlier fund of meanings as well.*[102]

From the above citation and all that this study has endeavoured to explain, one could immediately grasp that God included the ministry of his holy angels in the plan of saving man.

Our research on the ministry of the Angels is motivated primarily by the desire to discover what gift God has given to man in the service of the Angels. This too, I believe has motivated many researchers on the subject in the past and recent times.[103] What is most worthwhile rediscovering about the Angels is their considerable influence upon the natural order, and in particular in relation to the salvation of all the redeemed in Christ. Man is only a part of creation and the completeness of the human *creatureliness* is fulfilled in his relationship with other parts of creation – the Angels and the devils. Giudici in his research remarks that "It is

---

[100] Matthew 4:6
[101] Cf. Ex. 32, 34
[102] J. LANG. Op. cit. p. 141.
[103] M. P. GIUDICI, Op. cit. p. 14.

important to realize that the angels relate not only to what man is at the moment but also to what he will become. Thus, it is truly in no way useless to try to understand who the angels are, for what they have to teach us about their own mode of being reveals something about the mode of being towards which we are in some sense tending".[104]

Indeed there is reasonable ground to believe with Giudici that unless man strives with the cooperation of the Angels, we would be eternally separated from God.[105] God has planned for man in these holy ministers, an indispensable partnership if he must reach the Promised Land – Heaven.

4.3   Understanding Specific Charges of the Angels Concerning Man

In general, it would be practically an impossible task to discuss the ministry of the holy Angels in daily human exigencies because, "we cannot actually know how much they are doing. What we perceive or read about, we must believe to be only a tip of the iceberg."[106] Therefore, it would serve our purpose to follow few Scriptural lead on their ministry to man while acknowledging the testimonies of Christian tradition (Catholic) and other attested individual revelations.

In the Scriptures, it is the nature of the Angels to carry out divine will for man, both the wicked[107] and the godly. In the context of our text of study, our concern is with the godly.

Conversely, the ministry of the holy angels to the elect includes, *providing* for, *protecting, delivering, comforting* and *guiding*. I prefer to limit myself to these four generally in this part of the work. We will see more in the later part as we take the ranks individually. We will use few biblical instances to point out clearly how they perform these roles.

---

[104] Loc. cit.

[105] Ibid, p. 15.

[106] J. LANG, Op. cit. p. 142.

[107] Against sinners, God used them to destroy Sodom for its perversions (Genesis 19:1, 13); to curse Meroz because the people refused to help Israel (Judges 5:23); to bring pestilence upon Israel when David numbered them (II Samuel 24:15-17); to avenge those who persecute the saints (Psalm 35:5-6); and to kill Herod for not giving glory to God (Acts 12:23).

4.3.1 The Angels Provide

God has commanded his angels to provide for man in time of need. After the temptation of Jesus, Mt. 4, 11 reports that immediately the devil left, "the Angels came and served him ἴαγγελοι προσῆλθον καὶ διηκόνουν αὐτῷ)". This is reminiscent of Elijah's difficult journey of forty days and night to Horeb (1 Kings 19:5-6). As God commanded an Angel to provide bread for Elijah because the journey would be too difficult without eating (cf. 1 Kings 19:7), so does he command them still to provide for all his elect.

Angelic provision for man is not limited to bread.[108] In the earlier Church we have record of Angelic provision for the young Church.[109] They still provide for the Church today.

4.3.2 The Angels Protect and Deliver

In Matthew 4, 6 the devil cited Psalm 91, 11-12 for Jesus as the ground for him to jump from the pinnacle of the temple since God has commanded the Angels to protect him from harm. The wrong application notwithstanding, the picture is clear that even the devil knows that the Angels of God have the charge from the Lord to protect all the faithful.

In the OT, an Angel was sent to protect Daniel from the lions.[110]

In the NT, Peter was delivered with the assistance of an Angel from the intention of Herod to kill him after the Passover as he did to James already.[111] Further discussion on the ministry of protection received from the Angels would be given under *guiding* – particular role of Angel Guardian. God has commanded his Angels to protect his faithful in all their ways even today.

---

[108] In the widest sense, they are agents of god's providence (Cf. Ex. 12:23; 2 Sam. 24:16; 2 Kings 19:35; 1 Chr. 21:16; Ps. 104:4; Acts 12:23; 1 Cor. 10:10; Heb. 11:28)

[109] God provided deliverance from prison: 1. in the case of the twelve apostles (Acts 5:17-20); 2. in the case of peter (Acts 12:7-11).

[110] "My God sent His angel and shut the lions' mouths, so that they have not hurt me, because I was found innocent before Him; and also, O king, I have done no wrong before you" (Daniel 6:22).

[111] Cf. Acts 12:1-5.

4.3.3   The Angels Comfort

In the OT, an Angel was sent to comfort Hagar the slave-girl of Sarah in the wilderness and to give water to the crying little boy (cf. Gen. 21, 17).

The specific responsibility of assuring Paul that they would survive the tempest of the raging Sea on his way to Caesar in the NT was performed by God's angel (Acts 27, 24). God has commanded the Angels to comfort his faithful even today.

4.3.4   The Angel Guide or the Guardian Angel

In practical terms, the whole effort of our study is to arrive at this point of realization: that whoever runs to Yahweh for safety and makes the Most High his security, has the privilege of enjoying the charge of God's holy Angels especially the Guardian angels.

The ministry of Guardian Angels has been enjoyed by God's people from the OT. This summary from the Catholic Encyclopedia saves many words in explanation,

> *In the Bible this doctrine is clearly discernible and its development is well marked. In Genesis 28-29, angels not only act as the executors of God's wrath against the cities of the plain, but they deliver Lot from danger; in Exodus 12-13, an angel is the appointed leader of the host of Israel, and in 32:34, God says to Moses: "my angel shall go before thee." At a much later period we have the story of Tobias, which might serve for a commentary on the words of Psalm 90:11: "For he hath given his angels charge over thee; to keep thee in all thy ways." (Cf. Psalm 33:8 and 34:5) Lastly, in Daniel 10 angels are entrusted with the care of particular districts; one is called "prince of the kingdom of the Persians", and Michael is termed "one of the chief princes"; cf. Deuteronomy 32:8 (Septuagint); and Ecclesiasticus 17:17 (Septuagint).*

This sums up the Old Testament doctrine on the point; it is clear that the Old Testament conceived of God's angels as His ministers who carried out his behests, and who were at times given special commissions, regarding men and mundane affairs. There is no special teaching; the doctrine is rather taken for granted than expressly laid down; cf. II Machabees 3:25; 10:29; 11:6; 15:23. [112]

In a succinct way, the NT teaching on the Guardian Angels is summarized too,

Without dwelling on the various passages in the New Testament where the doctrine of guardian angels is suggested, it may suffice to mention the angel who succoured Christ in the garden, and the angel who delivered St. Peter from prison. Hebrews 1:14 puts the doctrine in its clearest light: "Are they not all ministering spirits, sent to minister for them, who shall receive the inheritance of salvation?" This is the function of the guardian angels; they are to lead us, if we wish it, to the Kingdom of Heaven. [113]

It would look repetitive reading through the long citation but it is for emphasis sake and to draw our attention that all the earlier proceedings move towards this teaching that the Angels have been commanded by God to guide his faithful to the Promised Land.

Mrs Caroll Cruz in her research found a list of charges these Angels have on their immediate wards:

1) They preserve us from many unknown dangers to soul and body.
2) They defend us against the temptations of the evil spirits.
3) They inspire us with holy thoughts and prompt us to deeds of virtue in the Divine service.
4) They warn us of spiritual dangers and admonish us when we have sinned.
5) They unite with us in prayer and offer our prayers to God.
6) They defend us at the hour of death against the last attacks of our spiritual foes.

---

[112] Catholic Encyclopedia, Op. cit., available online: http://www.newadvent.org/cathen/07049c.htm.
[113] Loc. cit.

7) They console the souls languishing in Purgatory and then conduct them to Heaven when their faults have been fully expiated. [114]

This would look like a list from a pious devotion book. Yet that is what has been the teaching of Christian faith especially among the Catholics: St. Thomas teaches[115] us that only the lowest orders of angels are sent to men, and consequently that they alone are our guardians, though Scotus and Durandus would rather say that any of the members of the angelic host may be sent to execute the Divine commands. Not only the baptized, but every soul that comes into the world receives a guardian spirit; St. Basil,[116] however, and possibly St. John Chrysostom[117] would hold that only Christians were so privileged. Our guardian angels can act upon our senses[118] and upon our imaginations – not, however, upon our wills, except "per modum suadentis",[119] viz. by working on our intellect, and thus upon our will, through the senses and the imagination.[120] Finally, when we die they are not separated from us, but accompany us to heaven, thus illustrating to us the fidelity of their angelic ministry – "*ad aliquam illustrationem*".[121]

Pope John Paul II in his General audience of 6 August 1986, gave a beautiful resume of all we have laboured to explore in this study arriving at the same point that man has a wonderful gift from God in these Angels and we should revere and invoke them. These are highlights from his homily:

1. God created both realities from the very beginning -- the spiritual reality and the corporeal, the earthly world and the angelic world. He created all this at one and the same time (simul) with a view to the creation of man, constituted of spirit and matter and set, according to the biblical narrative, in the framework of a world already established according to His laws and already measured by time (deinde).

---

[114] J. C. CRUZ, Op. cit., p. 123-124: She adapted this from the little booklet by an unknown author titled "*The Guardian Angels – Our Heavenly Companions*".
[115] (S. Th. I, 113:4).
[116] (Homily on Psalm 43).
[117] (Homily 3 on Colossians).
[118] (S. Th. I, 111:4).
[119] (S. Th. I, 111:3).
[120] (S. Th. I, 106:2; and I, 111:2).
[121] (S. Th. I, 108:7, ad 3am).

2. As creatures of a spiritual nature, the angels are endowed with intellect and free will, like man, but in a degree superior to him, even if this is always finite because of the limit which is inherent in every creature. The angels are therefore personal beings and, as such, are also "in the image and likeness" of God.

3. The ancient authors and the liturgy itself speak also of the angelic choirs (nine, according to Dionysius the Areopagite). Theology, especially in the patristic and medieval periods, has not rejected these representations, seeking to explain them in doctrinal and mystical terms, without, however, attributing an absolute value to them. Saint Thomas preferred to deepen his researches into the ontological condition, the epistemological activity and will into the loftiness of these purely spiritual creatures, both because of their dignity in the scale of beings and also because he could investigate more deeply in them the capacities and the activities that are proper to the spirit in the pure state, deducing no little light to illuminate the basic problems that have always agitated and stimulated human thought: knowledge, love, liberty, docility to God, how to reach His Kingdom. *The theme which we have touched on may seem "far away" or "less vital" to the mentality of modern man. But the Church believes that she renders a great service to man when she proposes sincerely the totality of the truth about   God   the   Creator   and   also   about   the   angels.*[122]

4. We find these experiences in various passages of Sacred Scripture, like for example, Ps. 90 which has already been quoted several times: "He will give His angels charge over you, to keep you in all your ways. On their hands they will bear you up, lest you dash your foot against a stone" (Ps. 90:11-12). Jesus Himself, speaking of children and warning against giving them scandal, refers to "their angels" (Mt. 18:10). Besides this, He attributes to the angels the function of witnesses in the last divine judgment about the fate of those who have acknowledged or denied Christ: "Whoever acknowledges me before men,

---

[122] Italics mine.

the Son of Man likewise will acknowledge him before the angels of God, but whoever denies me before men will be denied before the angels of God" (Lk. 12:8-9; cf. Rev. 3:5).

5. From these few facts which we have cited as examples, we understand how the Church could come to the conviction that God has entrusted to the angels a ministry in favor of people *Therefore the Church confesses her faith in the guardian angels, venerating them in the liturgy with an appropriate feast and recommending recourse to their protection by frequent prayer, as in the invocation "Angel of God."*[123] This prayer seems to draw on the treasure of the beautiful words of Saint Basil: "Every one of the faithful has beside him an angel as tutor and pastor, to lead him to life".[124]

---

[123] Italics mine

[124] JOHN PAUL II, *The Angels Participate in History of Salvation*, Catholic forum: General audience of 6 August, 1986, Online: http://www.catholic-forum.com/saints/pope0264fe.htm. Accessed on 21/02/2006. (cf. Saint Basil, Adv. Eunonium, III, 1; cf. also Saint Thomas, Summa Theol. I, q.11, a.3)

5.   CHAPTER FIVE

THE RANKS OF ANGELS AND THEIR MINISTRIES

After all above, let us see the Angels according to their ranks and ministry. My Catholic Catechism teaches me that those triumphant in heaven (Saints and Angels) form part of the Body of Christ – the Church.[125] But my Sacred Scripture teaches me that the earthly is always patterned or fashioned according to the Heavenly (cf. Ex. 25:9, 40; Acts 7:44; Heb. 8:5). The Angelic ranking is the prototype of most earthly spiritual kingdoms – the fallen angels.

We will discuss them according to the triadic arrangement of St. Thomas Aquinas as presented earlier.

5.1   ANGELS MINISTERING DIRECTLY TO GOD

The Angels of the first Triad are Thrones, Cherubim and Seraphim going from the outer to the inner Being of God. These are the Angels who are closest communicants of the glory and majesty of God. Through them the Spirit of God in its sublimity is communicated to the other Triads and to the created world. They are the most powerful Angels in the service of God. Let us take them one-by-one. As already indicated, they unceasingly adore and worship God.

5.1.1   The Thrones

In the book of Daniel 7: 9, Daniel was shown a vision where he saw the "Ancient of Days" seated on His "Throne". The Hebrew word used here for is כָּרְסֵא (*korse*). It is a word with

---

[125] The Basic Catholic Catechism Part Five: The Apostles' Creed IX-XII, art. 9: The Holy Catholic Church; the Communion of Saints.

Aramaic origin.[126] OT uses this word for 'thrones' severally to refer to kingly seats[127], especially ones with great authority.

In the context of the Angels, θρόνος (thronos) in Revelation 16:10 is used in singular as a substituted attribute (metonymy) of one who holds dominion or exercises authority. We find the same word used in the plural indicating the Angels' authority in Colosian 1:6:

> For in Him all things in heaven and on earth were created, things visible and invisible, whether Thrones or Dominions or Rulers or Powers – all things have been created through Him and for Him".

Revelation 4:2-5 gives us a clearer image of this rank of Angels as BEARERS of the seat of God.

> ...and behold, a throne was standing in heaven, and One sitting on the throne. And He who was sitting was like a jasper stone and a sardius in appearance; and there was a rainbow around the throne, like an emerald in appearance...And from the throne proceeds flashes of lightning and sounds and peals of thunder. And there were seven lamps of fire burning before the throne, which are the seven Spirits of God;

God radiates His goodness, His Love, His brilliance through the Thrones (including the Cherubic and Seraphic ranks). They are the stately pantheon of God.

The Thrones alone, as the outer layer of the Triad, are described to have the image of a shiny orb that shifts rainbow-like colors (cf. Rev 2:3). They are huge and are many-eyed, with six wings and often depicted in appearance as the "four beasts" (cf. Rev. 4:8). They act as the flaming chariot. As the outer layer of this Triad, the Thrones mark where the emanations of God begin to take on transitional forms from the interior sublimity of divinity only the Seraphims possess.

---

[126]H. M., BOUDON, Devotion to the Nine Choirs of Holy Angels, Especially to Angel-Guardians, London: Burns and Oates, 1911, p. 147.

[127] In the Septuagint, כָּרְסָא (korse) is a chair of state standing on a footstool. But N.T. in a metonymical sense assigns this chair alone to *kingly power or royalty*. Cf. Luke 1:32, 52; Acts 2:30. However, in other places, N. T. uses the same word in a metaphorical sense to refer to *God as the governor of the world*. Cf. Matt. 5:34; 23:22; Acts 7:49 (Is. 66:1); Rev. 1:4;3:21;4:2-6,9,10 etc; Heb. 4:16; 8:1; 12:2.

The specific ministry of the Thrones, as with Cherubim and Seraphim, is to adore God unceasingly: *"And day and night they do not cease to say, 'Holy, holy, holy is the Lord God, the Almighty, who was and who is and who is to come"* (Rev. 4:8). But in a special way, this rank is the judgment seat of God for pronouncing His divine Justice and administering His infinite Mercy. They ensure and maintain the divine energies in the disposition of judgments. In other words, this rank oversees how the justice of God is fulfilled in the world: They generate, direct and gather positive energies for divine justice. They make sure that justice is properly meted out and in cases where it is not, Angels from the Thrones send healing and consoling energies to victims while shining a light on injustice in order to attract our attention to it.

They are believed to possess great peace, utterly humble and submissive in spite of their majestic position. These qualities enable them to dispense divine justice objectively and with no trace of pride.

5.1.2   The Cherubim

The Hebrew word כרוב (*kerub*) has doubtful origin. Many biblical authorities[128] agree that the meaning of the root letters *KRB*, even in other languages, connote *One* who "Grips" or "Guards".

In this connection, S. Radabaugh writes

> *a CHERUB, in the context of heavenly beings, is a THRONE-GRIPPER, i.e. a THRONE-GUARDIAN, THRONE-COVERER, the Throne being that on which the Word of God sits in the Third Heaven. Collectively, the heavenly CHERUBIM comprise the guardians of the Throne in Heaven, or in rabbinical terms ... the innermost portion of His angelic Tallith with which He is pleased to wrap His Throne in Heaven, the innermost Shekhinah.*[129]

---

[128] Cf. Gesenius-Tregelles (GT) pp. 413-4; Brown-Driver-Briggs (BDB) pp. 500-501 and Companion Bible (CB) Appendix 41.
[129] S. E., RODABAUGH, The Angelic Ranks, Online article originally presented at *1991 Jumonville Conference, http://www.biblestudiesonline.info/TGF/topical/angelic_ranks.htm.* Accessed 29/07/11.

The Cherubims as Gripers or Guardians of the Shekkinah of God have OT instances. The Angels that were posted to 'guard' Eden after the expulsion of Adam from the garden were named *Cherubim* (cf. Gen 3:24). In other OT manifestations of Divine Presence, Cherubims featured as attendants of these theophanies. When God delivered Patriarch David from the hands of Saul in answer to his prayers, David declared in Ps. 18: 6-10:

> *In my distress I called upon the LORD; to my God I cried for help.*
> *From his temple he heard my voice, and my cry to him reached his*
> *ears… He bowed the heavens, and came down; thick darkness was*
> *under his feet. He rode on a cherub, and flew; he came swiftly*
> *upon the wings of the wind.*

Elsewhere in Ps 80:1; 99:1; 1 Sam 4:4, we find similar expressions of God as one who sits enthroned upon the Cherubim. In fact, from the OT uses of the term 'Cherub' (28 times) and Cherubim (68 times)[130] one gets four basic images of this rank:

1. They are pictured as living chariot of the theophanic God with the imagery of the storm-wind. Notice that in Ps.18:11 and 2 Sam. 22:11, the phrase "…and *he rode upon a Cherub* and flew swiftly on the wings of the wind", takes the expression of God riding on the chariot of clouds as in Psalm Ps. 104:3. The Hebrew word for chariot is '*rekhubh*' which is an inversion of '*kerubh*'.

2. They are pictured as gripping and guarding the throne of Yahweh Sabbaoth where the Ark of the Covenant is placed. (Cf. 1 Sam. 4:4; 2 Sam. 6:2 and I Chron. 13:6). In these passages, the context shows that the Ark of the Covenant are referred to, and it is probable that the same reference is found in 2 Kg. 19:15; Is. 37:16; Ps. 80:2 and Ps. 99:1.

3. In the book of Ezekiel (cf. 1:5; 9:3; 10:1, 22), one gets the impression that their image is interchangeable with those of the Seraphim.

In the NT visions of John the Apostle, the 'Seraphim' (שָׂרָף) of Isaiah 6:2, 6 are presented as another form of the Cherubim. The Apocalyptic description of them in the book of Revelation

---

[130] Bible Works, 6.0, sub verbum "Cherub" and "Cherubim".

in chapters 4-6 combines the expressions of four living creatures in 'Zoon' (ζῷον) as they are known in the Septuagint. S. Rodabaugh explains that the Greek word ZOON, plural ZOA, means LIVING ONE. The root emphasizes that the Cherubim, together with the Seraphim and the Thrones, are depicted in some way by land creatures.[131]

However, the peculiar quality of Angels from Cherubic choir is that they are Angels with great understanding or great effusion of wisdom. Through this choir deep knowledge of God and His mysteries are communicated to others. Through them, enlightenment is given to the spiritual eyes for seeing God. "More than the other lower orders of Angels, they are always radiant with the light of the knowledge of God, with the knowledge of the mysteries of God and the depths of His Wisdom; being themselves enlightened, they enlighten others."[132]

J. C. Cruz in her research confirms this, "Just as an intense love is attributed to the Seraphim, light and admirable knowledge are the possession of the Cherubim".[133] The Cherubim are Angels of divine Science. In their unceasing adoration of God, they receive the Divine Light and contemplate His splendor in a way more profound than others. It is their immersion in the luminous splendor of God that imparts in them "admirable knowledge, and holy effulgence with which they are replenished and is reflected in abundant streams upon the other hierarchies."[134]

What a strong divine atmosphere they create in union with the Seraphim in generating pure love and knowledge of God to the hierarchies and to entire creation! They are believed to be the guardians of light and of the stars. Though they are removed from human plane, the divine light that they filter down from the throne of God still touches human souls. From them, we arrive at the inner core of this Triad, the Seraphim.

---

[131] cf. S. E., RODABAUGH, op. cit
[132] S., DEMETRIUS, Orthodox Teachings on the Holy Angels, compiler, Online: http:www.ocf.org/OrthodoxPage/reading/angels.html. Accessed 29/07/11.
[133] J.C., CRUZ, ibid. p. 99.
[134] H. M. BOUDON, Opt. cit. p. 147.

5.1.3 The Seraphim

The Hebrew word 'Saraph' (שָׂרָף), plural 'Saraphim' means 'flaming'. Isaiah encountered the Seraphim in the OT as Angels of "fire" (cf. Is. 6:5-8). In his description of them, Isaiah saw them as Beings who attended upon Yahweh and have six wings (6:2), hands that held out a burning coal (6:6) and a voice that was calling out "Holy, Holy, Holy..." (6:3). They portray the image of God as fiery fire:

- In Moses' vision, "the appearance of the Lord was like a blazing fire" (Ex. 24:17)
- David knew God as One who "makes his Angels Spirits; his ministers a flaming fire" (Ps. 103:4).
- In Daniel's vision "His throne was a flame of fire" (Dan. 7:9).
- These Angels depict the aura of God as a "consuming fire" (Heb. 12:29)

The Seraphim are aflame with the fire of love for God. Their pure flame of love rekindles the ranks and the entire creation with divine love. Their flame lights (burns out) up darkness of evil as in the case of Isaiah and restores one to original state (Is. 6:7). For this, they are also guardians of *Truth* and preservers of *originality* of divine creation.

Their primary duty is to reverently wait on God in perpetual adoration of His profound goodness and love. They generate intense holiness of God which the Cherubim and Thrones resound and radiate onto the other ranks and upon all creation. Through the Seraphim more than the other ranks of the Angels, God communicates His love to His entire creation. Pure embers of God's love emanate from them to warm up every heart or soul looking up to God for the fulfillment of His holy will. We find this expressed in the writings of some of the fathers of the Church as J. C. Cruz reported[135] in her research: For St. Denis (d. 258), the Seraphim have eight fiery properties:

i.   Intense love – which is ever burning and consuming.
ii.   In constant motion – they are incessantly intent on God alone.
iii. Intensely hot – the Seraphic love is a burning love.
iv.   Fire that never loses its light – the Seraphic love abides in fullness

---

[135] J. C. CRUZ, op. cit., pp. 97-99.

v.	Fire that penetrates and permeates – it is combustible.
vi.	Transformative – fire that plunges and loses itself in the abyss of the divinity.
vii.	Communicative – transmits warmth and purifies.
viii.	The Seraphim pass on love and light into all the choirs of the Angels.

Dionysius, St. Gregory the great and St. Thomas Aquinas teach that the Seraphim are never sent out "for external earthly ministry". Although some like saint Francis of Assisi in his extraordinary experiences is believed to accept that they can be sent out in extraordinary situations.[136]

Besides, adoring God unceasingly; guarding the truth about God and inflaming creation with God's love, the Seraphim through singing the music of the spheres regulate the movement of the heavens as it emanates from God. And as such they radiate such a bright light that even other divine beings can hardly look upon their radiance. Of course, the Angels of the first Triad – Thrones, Cherubim and Seraphim – are more than what is described or written by any human being. They are better loved than known. Let us turn to the Angels of the second Triad.

5.2 ANGELS MINISTERING DIRECTLY TO NATURE (CREATED UNIVERSE).

Angels of the second Triad – Dominions, Virtues and Powers – as St. Thomas Aquinas teaches, have the responsibility of ministering directly or governing nature or the created universe.[137]

5.2.1 The Dominions

This choir of Angels is sometimes referred to as "Dominations". But 'dominations' as a word in plural never appeared in any biblical writings. It only appeared 3 times in the singular in the OT apocryphal book of 4Maccabees[138] with no lexical information.

---

[136] J. C. Cruz, op. cit. p. 98.
[137] S. Th. 1, 108
[138] Cf. 4Mac. 1:34; 3:18; 6:32

61

On the other hand, 'Dominion' in singular appeared 54 times in the biblical writings.[139] With the exception of the reference in Ephesians 1: 21, the other appearances referred to dominion as "power-over" or "ruler-ship-over" a subject. The New Revised Standard Version Bible translates different Greek words 'dominion' (cf. Rm 6:14 - κυριεύσει, Rm. 6:12 - βασιλευέτω, and 1 Tit. 6:16 - κρατος). In all these, Paul never used κυριότητος as he used in Ephesians 1:21. This same word κυριότητος, reappeared in the plural form in Colosians 1:6 (κυριότητες) in the context of one who possesses 'dominion' referring to the dominions, or power or lordship of Angels.[140] However, 'Dominations' has always been used interchangeably as a synonym to this choir of Angels. Both portrays a rank of Angels that rules as a sovereign.

Unlike the Angels of the first Triad, we have no biblical imagery of this choir. But customary pictures of them show them as wearing long albs, or gowns reaching to their feet, hitched with a golden belt and adorned with a green sole. They carry golden staffs in the right hand and the seal of God in the left. At other times, they are said to hold an orb or a scepter denoting their lordship over all created things.

From the writings of the early Fathers, especially that of Psuedo-Dionysius, we learn that the name given to the holy Dominions means, a certain unbounded elevation to that which is above, freedom from all that is terrestrial, and from all inward inclination to the bondage of discord, a liberal superiority to harsh tyranny, freedom from degrading servility and from what is low or base, because they are untouched by any inconsistency. In the words of St. Denis, "They are true lords, perpetually aspiring to true lordship and to the source of all lordship... They do not turn towards vain shadows, but wholly give themselves to that true authority, forever one with the godlike source of lordship".[141]

In summary, the Dominions are Angels combining spiritual and material order. They are known for their great intuition and wisdom as divine leaders. They champion the order of the law of cause and effect. They receive their immanence from the Seraphim and the Cherubim, or God Himself, and are responsible for ensuring that the cosmos remains in order. It is only with extreme rarity that they make themselves physically known to mortals. Instead, they quietly

---

[139] OT = 33x; NT = 11x; Apocryphal = 10x.

[140] Cf. κύριοι, 1 Cor. 8:5; see κύριος, at the end: Eph. 1:21; 2Pet. 2:10; Jude vs 8.

[141] Dionysius the Areopagite, *On the Celestial Hierarchies*, Transl. J. Parker, London, 1897, as found in Migne's *Patrologia Graeca*.

concern themselves with the details of existence. In this regard, they are often likened to act like "secretaries of state" to the great King – Jesus.[142]

5.2.2   The Virtues

We do not find explicit mentioning of the name of this choir of Angels either in the OT or NT. They are listed among the other ranks mentioned by St. Paul in Ephesians 1:21. Their origin is not quite clear.[143] Our strongest information about them is from the early Church Fathers' account. Concerning their rank, St. Denis indicates that "they have an equal order with the divine Dominations and Powers. They are so placed that they can perceive God in a harmonious and unconfused way and indicate the ordered nature of the celestial and intellectual authority, purification, illumination and perfection".[144]

Tradition refers to the Virtues as "shining ones" because they are pictured to have shapes like sparks of light.[145] They are Beings with radiant expression and they preside over the functioning of the universal elements – they govern and control the seasons, the stars, moon, the sun, the galaxies and the nebulae – all the celestial and terestial elements. They make sure that these elements are kept in their divinely appointed course and that evil forces do not manipulate them to any form of natural destruction.

The Virtues are also called 'Fortresses' or 'Strongholds' because they bolster the will for good within human hearts and instill stamina to follow sacred pathways by boosting the ability to remain steadfast with divine grace: *"They are as their name indicates personified power or virtue. God assigns them to such persons who strive unceasingly with all their soul to sanctify themselves, and who, even after they have successfully uprooted their failings, still continue to*

---

[142] Cf. H. M., BOUDON, op. cit. p. 144.
[143] Cf. J.C., CRUZ, op. cit. p.102.
[144] DIONYSIUS the Areopagite, loc. Cit.
[145] The nine choirs of the Angels, Catholic online article:
http://www.catholic.org/saints/anglchoi.php#virtues. Accessed 04/08/11.

apply all possible remedies of spiritual and corporal penance to make certain their eternal salvation".[146]

5.2.3 The Powers

The Greek word Δύναμις (*dunamis*) is a word in the Septuagint,[147] with a host of synonyms in the English translation. NRSV translated *dunamis* (powers) in several contexts to signify the *power* or *strength* or *ability* to perform miracles (cf. Mt. 25:15; 1 Cor. 12: 28f; 2 Cor. 1:8; 8:3). But the same word in another context personifies the *Power*, *Might*, or *Authority*. In an instance, the word refers to the Supernatural powers of God (cf. Mtt. 26:62; Mk. 14:62; Acts, 8:10), in another, it refers to the Angels (cf. Eph. 1:21) or to the Devil (cf. Lk. 10:19; 1 Cor. 15:24; 2 Pet. 2:11).

St. Paul used Δύναμις (dunamis) in Ephesians 1:21-22 to show that God has established Christ's powers over the power of Angels. But when St. Paul writes to the Roman (8:38): "*For I am sure that neither death, nor life, nor Angels, nor principalities, nor things present, nor things to come, nor Powers*", the *dunamis* here translated "*Powers*" is personified and stands in the same category with the "*angelos*" (angels) mentioned before them. The Powers St. Paul enumerated as the least among the forces here are believed to be the Angels who have fallen to become one of the cosmic powers at work against the sovereignty of Jesus Christ. In another place, St. Peter questioned: "*who has gone into heaven and is at the right hand of God with angels, authorities, and powers subject to him?*" In both instances, the meaning ascribed *dunamis* refers to the last choir of the second triad of Angels.

The Angels of this choir are pictured with the image of warriors because of their masculine and unshakable courage in all their activities.[148] They are also referred to as Potentiates or Authorities. From God – the Transcendent Power – they receive their powers like other Angels do. They are empowered as Angels of space and form to keep track of human history and to organize world religions. As St. Thomas said, their part in the governance of the

---

[146] The nine choirs of Angels section 1, Catholic online article:
http://www.catholictradition.org/Angels/angels10a.htm. Accessed 04/08/11.
[147] Cf. LXX Mt. 18: 24; 21:33; 25:15; Lk. 19:13 – *dunamis* signify 'strength', 'ability', 'power', 'might' or 'authority'.
[148] J.C., CRUZ, op. cit. p. 103.

universe is to carry out "what has been commanded".[149] Hence, they dispense justice and fight chaos. Their main work is like supernatural law agents (the Police):

> Powers have the task of defeating the efforts of the demons in overthrowing the world. They are declared awesome defenders of the cosmos against all evil and the maintainers of all cosmic order and equilibrium. They are the guardians of the heavenly paths, policing the routes to and from heaven to the earth. This means they concern themselves with humanity as well. The great harmonizers, they assist each soul to overcome the temptations placed before it to do evil and to lean instead toward the proper action (that being to Love and worship God).[150]

5.3   ANGELS MINISTERING DIRECTLY TO MAN

We have arrived at the last triad in the hierarchical grouping. Boudon writes concerning the ministry of this triad; "This last hierarchy is specially engaged in the care of men, of kingdoms, and of provinces, and of other things which peculiarly regard the good of men".[151] Precisely, this triad is the centre of my interest in the exposition of the work of the holy Angels. It is to them that Yahweh has *given a charge concerning man*. We begin with the Principalities.

5.3.1   The Principalities

NT writings used the Greek word – ἀρχή (arche) – to indicate *primacy*. But the same word is used in different contexts to mean three different things: For example, when St. Peter was narrating his vision at Joppa in Act 10:11, he used the word *arche* to describe the corners of the sheet that was lowered down to him. We find another instance in John 2:11 where the same

---

[149] S. Th. 1, 108.
[150] Cf. Powers, online article: http://www.circle-of-light.com/Angels/rank-powers.html. Accessed 05/08/11.
[151] H. M., BOUDON, op. cit. p. 127.

word (arche) was used by St. John to conclude Jesus' miracle at Cana indicating that the miracle marked the 'first' (*arche*) of other signs that Jesus manifested. In this instance, *arche* indicates 'first' as opposed to the others on the roll or the end (*telos*).[152] But in the letter of St. Paul to the Church at Ephesus (cf. 1:21) Paul used the same word *arche* to refer to the position or rank of power relating to a supernatural being or person with rule or domain or authority. Here, *archai* is translated 'Principalities'.

Hence, biblically the rank of Principalities points to a '*Primate*' or '*Primus*' in a *principality*, *kingdom* or *magistracy* with regards to office of being in charge. In the human realm or order, these Angels are entrusted with the principal or sovereign office.[153] Catholic Dictionary meaning of Principalities includes that these Angels take charge of countries and kingdoms too:

> Principalities are those angels who compose the highest choir in the lowest order of angels. With the archangels and angels, they constitute that heavenly multitude who are God's ordinary and immediate servants in the concerns of the visible world. It is probable, too, that to certain of the Principalities, God has assigned the care of countries and kingdoms.[154]

We do not have any biblical image of this choir of Angels. But traditionally, Principalities are described as Beings dressed in soldiers' uniform with golden girdles. St. Thomas lists them with the duties of executing the divine commands where he stated: "The execution of the angelic ministrations consists in announcing divine matter…leadership belongs to the Principalities".[155] It means that in the execution of angelic ministration, the Angels of this choir constitute the principal influence over the other choirs of the triad. St. Gregory and St. Denis think that the meaning of their name is based on this as J. C. Cruz cited in her book: "*The name of celestial Principalities signifies their Godlike princelines and authoritativeness in an order which is holy and most fitting to the princely powers, and that they are wholly turned towards the Prince of princes, and lead others in princely fashion*".

---

[152] Cf. similar uses in Mt. 24:8; Jn. 1:1; 6:64; 8: 25; 15:27 and Heb. 6:1.
[153] Cf. Thayer's Greek Lexicon in the BW 6.0, s.v. ἀρχή.
[154] Cf. New Catholic Dictionary, online: http:/www. Catholic-forum.com/saints/ncd06795.htm. Accessed 11/09/11.
[155] Cf. S. Th. 1, 108, 6:

When some of the Angels of this choir rebelled, they were cast from heaven and were believed to live in "the high places" or "in regions above" (cf. Eph. 6:2). Like the faithful Angels, these fallen angels preserved their ranks. The principalities among them constitute the major evil forces that fight the godly and pious people in their religious devotions.

The Principalities minister as 'caretakers' of nation, province, county, district, city, town and house. They work hand-in-hand with Guardian Angels to oversee spots or special places or events. In angelic bureaucracy, they are technically administrators for protection of co-operate bodies or institutions while the Guardian Angels protect individual bodies.

5.3.2   The Archangels

The name 'Archangel' appeared only in two places in the Bible (cf.1 Thes. 4:15 and Jude 1:9). In both places, the meaning clearly refers to a certain personage in the angelic ranks. Archangels form a special squad in the third triad because, of all the other ranks, they perform special ministry in the work of saving man. Originally, the Archangels come from the first triad. For instance, St. Michael is the prince of the Seraphim. But in ranking, he is placed on the second choir in the third triad as an 'archangel' because he serves as one of the Angels who minister to man in matters of graver moment. One unique factor about the Archangels is that they are Angels who can move directly from the presence of God into human affairs and vice versa. It is a special role granted only to them as Archangel Raphael declared to Tobit:

> *I was sent to test you. And at the same time God sent me heal you*
> *and Sarah your daughter-in-law. I am Raphael, one of the seven*
> *holy angels who present the prayers of the saints and enter into the*
> *presence of the glory of the Holy One* (Tobit 12:11-15).

One source has it that the travelling speed and manner of being-present of the Archangels is not common among the other ranks: "*An Archangel can travel from one end of the universe to the other in a second, and can be in many places at one time, even though these places may be millions of miles apart, like the light of the sun – appearing in several places at one time without its power lessoned in any of those spots*".[156] They are angels of special mission and they intervene in human history in grave moments to save man. To them God has entrusted the special role of protection and special love for all who are in crisis or times of grave need to protect and guard. They always bring great goodness and much happiness to those they are sent to. Take the biblical stories of Tobias or Daniel or Blessed Virgin Mary as good instances.

From the testimony of Archangel Raphael cited above their number is seven. This testimony agrees with the vision of St. John in Revelation 1:4; "*Grace to you and peace from him who is and who was and who is to come and from the seven spirits who are before his throne*". Though the Scripture agrees that the Archangels are seven in number, only Michael, Raphael and Gabriel have their special ministry to man explicitly recorded.

5.3.3   The Angels

In the New Revised Standard Version of the bible (the English version I have been quoting), the name "Angel" and "Angels" appeared 237 times and 103 times respectively. In these appearances, the name both in singular and plural make a general reference to divine messengers, that is, the whole ranks of the Angels. The entire eight ranks already discussed all serve as divine ministers to God; to natural order and to man but this last order, the ninth rank that bears the generic name of the whole ranks, serve man in a special way. To bring out their particular ministry to man they are called man's "Guardian Angels".

St. Thomas Aquinas specified the function of this last choir thus: "There are others who simply execute what is to be done; and these are the 'Angels'.[157] Through the lively presence of these Angels in the created world of man, God takes care of everything He has created in an individual and specific manner. St. Augustine is quoted to have said: "Everything visible in this

---

[156] Archangel, online article: http://www.geocities.com/Athens/Rhodes9813/archangle.html. Accessed 12/08/11.

[157] Cf. S, Th. 1, 108, 6.

world is put in charge of an Angel". Martin Luther asserts too that "God rules the world through the agency of his holy angels"[158]

Throughout the bible from the OT to the NT, numerous instances confirm the fact that every soul, every human being has a personal angel.[159] St. Jerome commented that what made the dignity of every soul so great is that each has "a guardian Angel from birth". To these guardian angels, God has given the charge of carrying out His own will for man's salvation (cf. Heb. 1:14). They have the task of mirroring in every little detail the goodness of God towards their ward (the souls under their charge). They not only take pleasure in serving the will of God as a special honor to them, but they show unbounded love for the soul they look after. Boudon expressed that the "loving charity of these blessed spirits toward men is so exceedingly great and so admirable, that we shall never be able to make any adequate return either of gratitude or homage".[160]

In the course of centuries, the Catholic Faithful have developed cult of the holy Angels to honor them and pray for their intercession. The earliest clear statement to pray to the Holy Guardian Angels is the words of St. Ambrose: "We should pray to the angels who are given to us as guardians".[161] Since then, as a general doctrine in the Catholic tradition, the Holy Angels have been accepted as a point of faith to be individuals' guardians. But from the time of St. Paul (cf. Col. 2:18) till now, the Catholic tradition has reprobated exaggerated cult of the Angels.[162]

The next part of my exposition will focus on testimonies of the saints on the ministry of these Holy Messengers and personal sharing of how they can still be of great help in our every day struggle with the things that derail us from the path of salvation.

---

[158] LLOYD, P. B., Angels in Tradition, online article: http://easyweb.easynet.co.uk/-ursa/angels/trad.htm. Accessed on 12/08/2011.

[159] Cf. Genesis 16:6-32, 24:7; 1 Kings 19:5; Judit 13:20; Psalm 33: Hosea 12:4; 8; Mt. 4:6; Acts 12:7.

[160] H. M., BOUDON, op. cit. p. 127.

[161] Cf. De Viduis, ix.

[162] Cf. CATHOLIC ENCYCLOPEDIA, online: http://www.newadvent.org/cathen/01476d.htm.

PART II

TESTIMONIES OF FAITH IN THE ANGELS

1. CHAPTER ONE – TESTAMENT ON THE ANGELS

1.1 INTRODUCTION – KEY NOTES OF THE FIRST PART

In case the reader has not read the first volume of this study on the Angels, I would like to reconnect him/her briefly to the flow of the presentation, believing in the opportune time, he/she will search for the details.

The first chapter dealt with finding the root of the English appellation 'Angel' in the Bible. After a long trace, it concluded that:

> The Septuagint,[163] following the Classical Greek usage makes no distinction between the human and divine messengers in translating mal'ak from the Hebrew to Greek. In general, it translates all to ángelos. Whereas the Latin rendering of this translation in the Vulgate distinguishes between nuntius (a messenger sent by man) and angelus (one sent by God).[164] Thus, the English translation from the Vulgate follows the distinction making the references clearer than the Septuagint. However, this back grounding is to help the reader to understand that when the term angel(s) is used in this work, one has to bear in mind that we are referring to angelus (angeli) – messenger(s) sent by God for a mission.

---

[163] The Septuagint or LXX refers to the Greek translation of the Old Testament writings used by the Jewish Hellenes (that is, Jews who lived in Greek world and could no longer read Hebrew language well). The translation which was believed to have been done by seventy Jewish scholars earned it the name 'Septuagint' or 'LXX'.

[164] M., FREEDMAN, Op. Cit., p. 309.

Then Chapter Two took up the task to find out who these messengers (*ma'lakim elohim*) are; giving the biblical presuppositions about their creation and existence; citing instances in the Bible predicating their nature, activities and showing how the traditional Catholic theology organizes them into hierarchy and ranks.

Chapter Three started with contextualizing the charge given to these *Heavenly Messengers* by God concerning man in Psalm 91:11 and ends in exposing the triadic ministry they perform according to the exposition of St. Denis. In the same connection, Chapter Four, further, through exegesis of some texts, technically illustrates God's love *concerning* man in *commanding* the Angels to serve man.

The Fifth Chapter exposed the service these Angels render to God, nature and man according to their ranks. The reader needs to know these Angels according to their ranks and their specific ministry. The technical nature of the first part, balances the pious nature of this part. Both are complementary and needs to be completely assimilated.

1.2 LIVE TESTIMONIES OF ANGELS IN THE BIBLE

1.2.1 Hebrew Testament

It is interesting to note that until the sixteenth chapter of the book of Genesis, the word 'Angel' was never used to picture any of the divine *theophanies* or manifestations. God posted the *Cherubim* with flaming sword to guard the tree of Life (Gen. 3:24). Remember as we already demonstrated[165], the Cherubim are the Angels through whom divine knowledge flows. You can understand why they are the ones to guard the tree of knowledge of good and evil. As at that time, one can probably assume that their ministry to God was not far removed from their service to man because the gap created by the sin of our first parents was still immediate. If before the fall, it was normal for Adam and Eve to sit together with God in the cool of the evening (Gen 3:8), Adam and Eve should be very familiar with the sight of the Angels of the first triad

---

[165] Confer sub number 6.1.2 of Part I on the Angels of the First Triad, s.v. *Cherubim*.

(Thrones, Cherubim and Seraphim). The Bible here shows how God uses the Angel particularly *in-charge* of that area of His creation as His *Messenger* in interacting with man.

We will cite two more striking testimonies of the Angels in the Hebrew Scripture as contained in the Bible. As we go through these stories, we put the service or the ministry of the Angels mentioned in these testimonies into their perspective ranks. The amazing discovery is that God maintains order in His creation.

1.2.1.1 Balaam, the Donkey and the Angel

In the story of Balaam the Seer (Num. 22-24), particularly in 22:20-35, we read:

> *That night God came to Balaam and said to him, "If the men have come to summon you, get up and go with them; but do only what I tell you to do." So Balaam got up in the morning, saddled his donkey, and went with the officials of Moab. God's anger was kindled because he was going, and the angel of the Lord took his stand in the road as his adversary. Now he was riding on the donkey, and his two servants were with him. The donkey saw the angel of the Lord standing in the road, with a drawn sword in his hand; so the donkey turned off the road, and went into the field; and Balaam struck the donkey, to turn it back onto the road. Then the angel of the Lord stood in a narrow path between the vineyards, with a wall on either side. When the donkey saw the angel of the Lord, it scraped against the wall, and scraped Balaam's foot against the wall; so he struck it again. Then the angel of the Lord went ahead, and stood in a narrow place, where there was no way to turn either to the right or to the left. When the donkey saw the angel of the Lord, it lay down under Balaam; and Balaam's anger was kindled, and he struck the donkey with his staff. Then the Lord opened the mouth of the donkey, and it said to Balaam, "What have I done to you, that you have struck me these*

*three times?" Balaam said to the donkey, "Because you have made
a fool of me! I wish I had a sword in my hand! I would kill you
right now!" But the donkey said to Balaam, "Am I not your donkey,
which you have ridden all your life to this day? Have I been in the
habit of treating you this way?" And he said, "No." Then the Lord
opened the eyes of Balaam, and he saw the angel of the Lord
standing in the road, with his drawn sword in his hand; and he
bowed down, falling on his face. The angel of the Lord said to him,
"Why have you struck your donkey these three times? I have come
out as an adversary, because your way is perverse before me. The
donkey saw me, and turned away from me these three times. If it
had not turned away from me, surely just now I would have killed
you and let it live." Then Balaam said to the angel of the Lord, "I
have sinned, for I did not know that you were standing in the road
to oppose me. Now therefore, if it is displeasing to you, I will
return home." The angel of the Lord said to Balaam, "Go with the
men; but speak only what I tell you to speak." So Balaam went on
with the officials of Balak* (**NRSV**).

Now, re-reading verses 20-23 very carefully, one wonders why the same God who
appeared to Balaam, the Seer, the previous night commanding him to go with the officials sent
by Balak king of Moab, now sends an Angel with a sword to block his road. There may be many
interpretations to this. One of which is that God sees the heart of Balaam getting enticed by
riches and honour to be received from the king of Moab as he (Balaam) conversed with the
officials on the way. Balaam though a Seer, cannot see God or His Angels unless he interiorly
communicates through the rites and prayers that put him on the realm of receiving divine
revelations. Moving along with the nobles and high officials of Balak (22:15), the man of God
who should be interiorly conversing with God and intently focused on carrying out the Lord's
command has turned attention to the exterior and its material lures and proposals of these nobles.
So, since the Lord cannot get his attention anymore, and if left without warning, he might end up
cursing the People he was supposed to bless. God intervened through the service of His holy

Angel. Anyone can disagree with this interpretation but no one can disagree that an Angel intervened.

The particular Angel sent by God, as seen by the donkey (and later Balaam), is an Angel from the second triad, from the rank of *Powers*: in verse **23**, *The donkey saw the angel of the Lord standing in the road, with a drawn sword in his hand...* From the biblical imagery and the exposition we made in volume 1 on the ministry of Angels according to their ranks, an Angel with a drawn sword should be from the rank of *Powers*. Relating this Angel with the Angel of Joshua 5:13-15, one cannot biblically be wrong to conclude that the Angel that stopped the donkey is from one of the heavenly army or warriors. Remember in the first part of our study we said that Angels belonging to this rank are "empowered as Angels of space and form to keep track of human history and to organize world religions"[166]. They are the heavenly law enforcement agents (the Police) that God uses to enforce divine order over human perversion. St. Thomas teaches that to them belongs the work of carrying out what God has commanded.[167] Pay attention to what the Angel said to Balaam when he saw him in verses 32-33:

> *"Why have you struck your donkey these three times? I have come out as an adversary, because your way is perverse before me. The donkey saw me, and turned away from me these three times. If it had not turned away from me, surely just now I would have killed you and let it live."*

A lot could be learnt from this biblical story, but I chose to point the story out as one of the Hebrew Testament's account of how Angels minister to man in their service to God according to their ranks. Some people may think that the story is one of the folklores told to foothold divine interventions in human affairs, but does that make the Angels not real? Fortunately, their real existence does not depend on what an individual is thinking or believing, thanks to God for that.

---

[166] Cf. 6.2.3 s.v. *Powers*.
[167] *Summa Theologica* 1, 108.

1.2.1.2 Manoah, Wife, and the Angel

Another interesting story of Hebrew Testament could be found in the book of Judges 13: 2-23;

> There was a certain man of Zorah, of the tribe of the Danites,
> whose name was Manoah. His wife was barren, having borne no
> children. And the angel of the Lord appeared to the woman and
> said to her, "Although you are barren, having borne no children,
> you shall conceive and bear a son. Now be careful not to drink
> wine or strong drink, or to eat anything unclean, for you shall
> conceive and bear a son. No razor is to come on his head, for the
> boy shall be a nazirite to God from birth. It is he who shall begin
> to deliver Israel from the hand of the Philistines." Then the woman
> came and told her husband, "A man of God came to me, and his
> appearance was like that of an angel of God, most awe-inspiring; I
> did not ask him where he came from, and he did not tell me his
> name; but he said to me, "You shall conceive and bear a son. So
> then drink no wine or strong drink, and eat nothing unclean, for
> the boy shall be a nazirite to God from birth to the day of his
> death.' " Then Manoah entreated the Lord, and said, "O Lord, I
> pray, let the man of God whom you sent come to us again and
> teach us what we are to do concerning the boy who will be born."
> God listened to Manoah, and the angel of God came again to the
> woman as she sat in the field; but her husband Manoah was not
> with her. So the woman ran quickly and told her husband, "The
> man who came to me the other day has appeared to me." Manoah
> got up and followed his wife, and came to the man and said to him,

*"Are you the man who spoke to this woman?" And he said, "I am."
Then Manoah said, "Now when your words come true, what is to
be the boy's rule of life; what is he to do?" The angel of the Lord
said to Manoah, "Let the woman give heed to all that I said to her.
She may not eat of anything that comes from the vine. She is not to
drink wine or strong drink, or eat any unclean thing. She is to
observe everything that I commanded her." Manoah said to the
angel of the Lord, "Allow us to detain you, and prepare a kid for
you." The angel of the Lord said to Manoah, "If you detain me, I
will not eat your food; but if you want to prepare a burnt offering,
then offer it to the Lord." (For Manoah did not know that he was
the angel of the Lord.) Then Manoah said to the angel of the Lord,
"What is your name, so that we may honor you when your words
come true?" But the angel of the Lord said to him, "Why do you
ask my name? It is too wonderful." So Manoah took the kid with
the grain offering, and offered it on the rock to the Lord, to him
who works wonders. When the flame went up toward heaven from
the altar, the angel of the Lord ascended in the flame of the altar
while Manoah and his wife looked on; and they fell on their faces
to the ground. The angel of the Lord did not appear again to
Manoah and his wife. Then Manoah realized that it was the angel
of the Lord. And Manoah said to his wife, "We shall surely die, for
we have seen God." But his wife said to him, "If the Lord had
meant to kill us, he would not have accepted a burnt offering and a
grain offering at our hands, or shown us all these things, or now
announced to us such things as these.*

First of all, the Israelites were under terrible sufferings for forty years in the hand of the Philistines. Unlike the case of the Midianites (Jdg 6:7), here the Bible did not tell us that the Israelites cried to the Lord to send them help. We know that the righteous remnants, presumably, would always be calling on Yahweh for help. But God took the initiative of sending his Angel to a family that was not expecting any visitation. This emphasizes the sovereign power of God's will and His boundless love to save man through the service of his heavenly Messengers. Notice that the Angel did not appear to the man of the house, but the wife. And, of course, the wife did not know what to do with the Messenger, so she reported to the husband who interceded with God to resend the Messenger.

Let us analyze Manoah's reaction. What if Manoah tells her wife; "You are hallucinating because you are desperate about a child"? A good number of men today will probably say that. Or what if Manoah is such a gentleman that he does not want to hurt her wife's feelings and apathetically says "ok, if you say you are sure of what you saw, that's fine with me! Only do not say it to someone else outside". In both cases, he would not care to pray God to resend the Angel. Only a man of faith, who believes in God and in His Angels like Manoah will beg God to resend the Angel. The Bible tells us that God answered his prayer and re-sent the Angel. Angels come to those who believe! No one should forget that God's initiative to save man needs man's faith and co-operation with His saving plan.

Secondly, from this biblical account, from what rank could this Angel come from? I would say that given the fact that this Angel came directly from divine initiative, (confer another instance in the Gospel of Luke 1:19) to one who was not at the moment expecting a visitation, and because of the weight of deliverance the child announced would carry out, the Angel must be from the rank of the Archangels. Strong support to this claim comes from the fact that the Angel rose and disappeared with the flames of the sacrifice:

> When the flame went up toward heaven from the altar, the angel of the Lord ascended in the flame of the altar while Manoah and his wife looked on; and they fell on their faces to the ground (Jdg, 13:20).

This means that this Angel is from the Seraphic Choir. The Archangels are the *Seraphims* who can easily appear in human form to deliver divine message or service. These Seraphic presence are sometimes taken in the Hebrew account as God himself. Look at the instances of Genesis 16:7; 22:11; 31:11; Exodus 3:2; 14:19; Judges 2:1; 6:11-24; Zechariah 3:1-6. In these instances, although they appear physically as Angels, their theophanic presence, utterances, and authority, are God's. Only the rank of Angel closest to God can take that form of appearance. However, remember the essential point here is not the argument from what rank the Angel comes, but the fact that God ministers to man through the service of an Angel.

1.2.1.3 Other References of Angels in the Hebrew Testament

Probably the reader would like to read from the Scriptures these chronicles of Angel's activities with our Patriarchs:

1. **Hagar** and **Ishmael** – Were delivered from death in the desert through the help of an Angel of the Lord (Gen. 16:1-16).
2. **Lot** – With her two daughters were saved from Sodom by an Angel (Gen.19: 1-25).
3. **Isaac** – Was saved by an Angel from being sacrificed by his father, Abraham, at Moriah (Gen 22: 1-18).
4. **Jacob** – Encountered the Angels twice (Gen. 28:12 and 32:1)
5. **Moses** – Received the Ten Commandments and an Angel to lead the Israelites into the promise land (Ex. 23:20-21).
6. **Joshua** – Saw and followed an Angel Commander sent to lead the company of Israelites into the promise land (5:13-15).
7. **Gideon** – Was encouraged by an Angel to fight and conquer the Madianites (Judg. 6:11-24).
8. **The prophets** – Elijah, Isaiah, Ezekiel, Zacharia – Were led by Angels (cf. 1 Kgs 18:39, 19:1-8, 2 Kgs 2:11; Is. 6:1-8; Ezk 1:4-2:1; Zech 1:8-2:2).

Our Fathers in the faith, lived and believed in the Angels, and it was well with them. Do we need to live and believe in the demons instead of the Angels? The book of Hebrews 13:7 advised us to consider the way our Fathers in the faith lived and imitate their faith in the Angels.

1.2.2   Christian Era – The Apostolic Testament

In the first part of our study, we cited biblical mention of the Angels in the New Testament writing. Here we simply want to tell the Angels' story as they were narrated in the early Christian tradition. In the whole of the NT, only in three places were the specific names and identity of the Angel mentioned; Archangels Gabriel (in Luke 1:26-38) and Michael (in Jude 9, Rev. 12:7). Besides these two clearly named, other appearances of the Angels did not show much of their identity and personality. They simply delivered their message or performed their service.

1.2.2.1 St. Peter's Experience

Peter's story did not occur later than 64 AD. In the story, an Angel delivered the Apostle Peter from what Herod planned for him according to Acts 12: 5-11:

> *While Peter was kept in prison, the church prayed fervently to God for him. The very night before Herod was going to bring him out, Peter, bound with two chains, was sleeping between two soldiers, while guards in front of the door were keeping watch over the prison. Suddenly an angel of the Lord appeared and a light shone in the cell. He tapped Peter on the side and woke him, saying, "Get up quickly." And the chains fell off his wrists. The angel said to him, "Fasten your belt and put on your sandals." He did so. Then he said to him, "Wrap your cloak around you and follow me." Peter went out and followed him; he did not realize that what was happening with the angel's help was real; he thought he was seeing a vision. After they had passed the first and the second guard, they came before the iron gate leading into the city. It opened for them of its own accord, and they went outside and walked along a lane, when suddenly the angel left him. Then Peter came to himself and said, "Now I am sure that the Lord has sent his angel and rescued me from the hands of Herod and from all that the Jewish people were expecting."*

As already mentioned, one could hardly identify from the story the personality of the Angel that visited Peter. But when the whole context of our study is put together, we can point to the rank of this Angel. Three factors clarify our context. First, Peter was in prison and needed release. Second, the Christian community is in fervent intercession for him, begging God to set him free and, thirdly, the Angel's appeared with 'light' and extraordinary 'radiance'. Verse 7 says, "*Suddenly an angel of the Lord appeared and a light shone in the cell*". Putting all these together, this Angel must be from the second hierarchy – from the rank of Virtues. Remember in our earlier study, we identified them as Angel of 'stronghold' invoked to sustain the stamina and the strong will to persevere in doing good:

> *The Virtues are also called 'Fortresses' or 'Strongholds' because they bolster the will for good within human hearts and instill stamina to follow sacred pathways by boosting the ability to remain steadfast with divine grace*[168]

We already had sample of the intercession of this faithful early Christian community in Act 4:23-31, where "*they raised their voices together to God and said... For in this city, in fact, both Herod and Pontius Pilate, with the Gentiles and the peoples of Israel, gathered together against your holy servant Jesus, whom you anointed, to do whatever your hand and your plan had predestined to take place. And now, Lord, look at their threats, and grant to your servants to speak your word with all boldness...*" The bible tells us that when they prayed, the housed they were staying in was shaken, and they were filled afresh with the Holy Spirit that gave them the boldness to continue their evangelization. Following this context, you can understand that their prayer for Peter's deliverance was to overcome still the evil plot of Herod and to continue the good course of evangelization. The Sovereign Angels responsible for maintaining good course and forestalling evil from over-taking a good course are the Virtues. Hence, I believe the Angel that delivered Peter in our story is from the Virtues. Are these biblical experiences of our forefathers in the faith not true? Angels are real according to the Testament of the early Christians.

---

[168] Confer sub-number 6.2.2 in Part I under the "Virtues".

1.2.2.2   St. Stephen's Experience

Earlier on, before Peter was arrested and put in the prison, we have the story of the first Martyr, Stephen. While the members of the Sanhedrin were accusing Stephen of blasphemy, the bible reported that they noticed something strangely extraordinary with him; "*And all who sat in the council looked intently at him, and they saw that his face was like the face of an Angel*" (Acts 6:15). The question is: why would the face of one facing death charges be brilliant like that of an Angel? Could it be that one of the Virtues is at work again? One would believe the answer is yes. Only that in Stephen's case, the Angel did not come to deliver him from dying but to strengthen and console him as an Angel did to Jesus at the garden of Gethsemane (cf. Lk 22:43). The Angel's reflection was shining on the face of St. Stephen. His murderers could not see the Angel, but they could see the reflection of his presence on Stephen's face. The Angel gave St. Stephen the boldness to speak out; made him pray for those who were stoning him and drew the veil blinding man from the glory of heaven so that Stephen could see where he was going and how ready the Master, Jesus, who should be *seated* at God's right hand (cf. Mk 16:19, Heb. 10:12), is now *standing* (Acts 6: 55-56) waiting to receive him. Surely, St. Stephen could not have been alone and be able to accomplish what he did at such grave moment. Heavenly presence and heavenly Messengers were with him. The Angel at work here, if you ask me, should be from the rank of Virtues, as we explained in Peter's case.

God can deliver us from death and imprisonment, if He wants, through his Angels. When, on the contrary, God thinks He is ready to receive us, He prepares us and assists us to overcome pain and death through the ministry of His holy Angels. The Angels are all over us working but we do not notice them because our minds are distracted by the material world.

1.2.2.3   St. Paul's Experience

We have another interesting apostolic Angel experience in the life of St. Paul before 68AD. St. Paul, as a prisoner, was boarded on a ship bound to Rome in the company of others (Acts 27:1-20). He warned the Centurion in-charge of the trip of grave dangers but the Centurion insisted on the journey (27: 9-12). When the journey got so difficult in the sea that all feared they would perish, helped by an Angel visitation, St. Paul reassured them,

> *Men, you should have listened to me and not have set sail from Crete and thereby avoided this damage and loss. I urge you now to keep up your courage, for there will be no loss of life among you, but only of the ship. For last night there stood by me an angel of the God to whom I belong and whom I worship, and he said, 'Do not be afraid, Paul; you must stand before the emperor; and indeed, God has granted safety to all those who are sailing with you.' So keep up your courage, men, for I have faith in God that it will be exactly as I have been told".*

From the above story, we would like to re-emphasize a couple of points; first, there were many other prisoners in the ship (27:1). Remember, verses 5-6 of our story said *"After we had sailed across the sea that is off Cilicia and Pamphylia, we came to Myra in Lycia. There the centurion found an Alexandrian ship bound for Italy and put us on board"*. The ship was a big one and many people were on board. Of course, the presence of a centurion of Augustan Cohort (27:1) means already that a cohort of soldiers were with him, not counting other travelers on business or personal trip to Italy. Of all these people on board, only St. Paul was sure they would survive because an Angel stood by him. Others have given up as the story confirmed in verse 20: *"When neither sun nor stars appeared for many days, and no small tempest raged, all hope of our being saved was at last abandoned"*. St. Paul believed in the Angels and honoured them as one to whom he belongs (27:23). That was why in the moment of such darkness, the Angel's light and presence provided him sure hope. St. Paul reassured fellow travelers, *"So keep up your courage, men, for I have faith in God that it will be exactly as I have been told"*. I can still hear St. Paul telling us, today, to believe in the Angels and keep our faith that their ministry to us will help us always in hopeless moments.

Second emphasis, who could that "Angel-who-*stood by me*" in St. Paul's account be? One would believe it should be his Guardian Angel because the Angel had been with him all the time, otherwise, how could he had known beforehand that the travel will be dangerous and had warned the Centurion (27:10-11)? This Angel Guardian stood by Paul and ministered to him, instructing, consoling, strengthening and continually revealing the mysteries of God (2 Cor. 12:4), and of the mission ahead (Acts 27:24). Remember that it is from St. Paul's writing that we got the names of the ranks of the Angel before St. Denis put them into hierarchies. How did he get these revelations if the Holy Messengers of God were not with him? The big question is: where were the Guardian Angels of all others in the ship? Does it mean that they do not have them? Or they were not communicating with their own Guardian Angels? One would think the later answer is the case.

1.3   THE CHURCH FATHER'S TESTAMENT

The Apostolic testament given above did not exceed the period of AD 100. The next period of the Christian faith, the Church Fathers, spanned from AD 100 up to 451 (Council of Chalcedon). Some theologians extend Patristic period up to the 8th century. My interest is to pick the teachings of few of these Church fathers to show that they believed in the Angels and had experienced them too.

St. Ignatius of Antioch (ca 35-107) and Clement of Rome (ca 96 AD) were post-Apostolic Fathers. They experienced the post-Paschal Christians community. St. John the Evangelist made Ignatius a bishop.[169] Ignatius wrote to the Trullians concerning the Angels and heavenly mysteries,

> *For even I, though I am bound (for christ), and am able to understand heavenly things, the angelic orders, and the different sorts of angels and hosts, the distinctions between powers and dominions, and the diversities between the thrones and authorities,*

[169]Epistle of Ignatius to the Trullians, "The Ante-Nicene Fathers", Vol 1, Grand rapids Michigan: Wm. B. Eerdmans Publishing Co, 1956, p. 68.

> *the mightiness of Aeons, and the pre-eminence of the Cherubim*
> *and Seraphim, the sublimity of the spirit, the Kingdom of the lord,*
> *and above all, the incomparable majesty of the Almighty God–*
> *though I am acquainted with these things, yet am I not therefore by*
> *any means perfect...* [170]

Ignatius said he understood these things well but he feared to write these mysteries to the Trullians whom he considered "babes" in such matters. I think everyone should be told about the Angels even if he decides not to believe in them. That is what we are doing here.

Likewise, St. Clement of Rome who was baptized by St. Peter the Apostle became Peter's disciple and later succeeded St. Peter as the third Pope of Rome. He wrote about the Angels:

> *Let us think of the whole host of angels, how they stand by and*
> *serve his will, for Scriptures say: "Ten thousand times ten thousand*
> *were doing service to him, and they cried out: Holy, holy, holy,*
> *Lord Sabaoth; the whole of creation is full of His glory." Then let*
> *us gather together in awareness of our concord, as with one mouth*
> *we shout* [171]

The Holy Father advises us to "to gather together in awareness of our concord..." in the ministry and service of these Holy Messengers of God.

Other Church Fathers, Clement of Alexandria (ca 150-250 AD)[172], Origen (ca 185-254 AD)[173] and Shepherd of Hermas (an unknown author of the second century considered on equal level with the canons of the Scriptures) all teach on the Angels. Shepherd of Hermas teaches that

---

[170] ibid. p. 68.
[171] Saint Clement of Rome, "Epistle to the Corinthians," XXXIV, *The Early Christian fathers*, ed. and trans. by Henry Bettenson, Geoffrey Cumberledge. Oxford: Oxford University Press, 1956, p. 47.

[172] The Stromata of Miscellanies, in the Ante-Nicene Fathers, Vol 1, p 524.
[173] De Principiis, Chapter VIII – On the Angels, pp 265-266.

every man has an Angel and a demon that follows him. If any man listens to the Angel, he behaves well (righteous) but if he listens to the demon, he becomes bad (evil):

> There are two angels with a man – one of righteousness, and the other of iniquity." And I said to him, "How, sir, am I to know the powers of these, for both angels dwell with me?" "Hear," said he, and "understand them. The angel of righteousness is gentle and modest, meek and peaceful. When, therefore, he ascends into your heart, forthwith he talks to you of righteousness, purity, chastity, contentment, and of every righteous deed and glorious virtue. When all these ascend into your heart, know that the angel of righteousness is with you. These are the deeds of the angel of righteousness. Trust him, then, and his works. Look now at the works of the angel of iniquity. First, he is wrathful, and bitter, and foolish, and his works are evil, and ruin the servants of God. When, then, he ascends into your heart, know him by his works."[174]

The Pastor of Hermas wants to appreciate the fruits these Holy Angels produce in us through their presence. Likewise, the demons in us show themselves through evil works. This is a true fact and not imagination. One may need to stop a moment and reflect: which of these spirits control one's life more and why? What one believes in takes control of him more!

It will increase one's faith to read up the footnote references to the testaments of later Fathers, St. Athanasius (ca 296-373 AD),[175] St. Basil the Great (ca 330-379 AD),[176] St. Gregory of Nyssa (330-395 AD),[177] St. Gregory Nazianzen (329-391 AD),[178] St. Cyril of Jerusalem,[179] St. Ambrose (ca 339-397 AD),[180] St. Augustine of Hippo (ca 354-430 AD) and St. John

---

[174] The Pastor of Hermas, in the Ante-Nicene Fathers, Vol II. p. 266.

[175] Discourse II Against the Arians, Chapters XVII in Nicene and Post-Nicene Fathers, series II, Vol 1, p 362.

[176] The Hexameron, Homily 1,5, Nicene and Post Nicene Fathers, Series II, Vol VIII, p54.

[177] On the Soul and the Resurrection, in Nicene and Post-Nicene Fathers, Series II, Vol V, p. 103.

[178] Oration XXXVIII, IX-X, On the Theophany or Birthday of Christ, Nicene and Post-Nicene Fathers, Series II, Vol VII, p 347.

[179] Lectures III-XV, 3-24, p 14-111.

[180] Exposition of the Christian Faith, Book III, Chapter 3, p 245.

Chrysostom[181] all taught or wrote about the Angels. These forefathers in our faith were able to live holy and exemplary lives through their faith in God and the ministry of His Holy Messengers, the Angels. It is over two thousand years since they all passed away, but their good life, good work, and writings remain with us. Believing in what works and what endures is always a better option.

---

[181] Homilies on Hebrews, III, p 377.

2.   CHAPTER TWO

THE SAINTS AND ANGELS' STORIES

In the first part of our study on the Angels, we saw from the Bible that the Angels exist and serve as God's Messenger to man. We pointed out through biblical texts and narratives that their activities are Scriptural and not mere imagination. In the first chapter of the second part, we have also pointed to Ancient and later testaments' stories, testimonies and writings in the Scriptures and from our fore-founders in the Christian faith that Angels are real. Now, in this chapter, I will recount some of the existing and well-known stories of famous Saints and their interaction with the Holy Angels. Do not forget that these stories are retold briefly with the intention of eliciting the readers' interest in the Angels. Full and detailed accounts of the stories may be found in the footnoted references or other reliable Christian writings.

2.1   St. Francis of Assisi and a Seraph

There are many biographies of St. Francis of Assisi one can read about this extraordinarily gifted man of God. Here, we will point out few things in his early life, his boyhood, and finally his religious experiences culminating in the encounter with a Seraph that gave him the wounds of a stigma.

When Francis was born in 1182, her mother named him John the Baptist. When his father returned from his business trip from France (he was a cloth merchant dealing with textiles and fabrics), not wanting anything of God to do with his boy, he renamed the boy "Francesco" (which meant a Frenchman). Pietro Bernardone, his father, wanted *Francesco* to take after him. Francis grew up after his father, indulgent with the lives of nobles – living in all kinds of permissiveness, habituated to evil and used to vice. He himself later confessed, "I lived in sin".

Francis' conversion came when he was on the way to a war that could have earned him the much-coveted honour of being a knight. Francis dreamt, after the first day's journey to the battle, that God wanted him to return home. He returned, to the greatest displeasure of his father and utter humiliation among his friends and countrymen. He suffered terribly at the hands of his father who felt completely disappointed in him. His father made Francis to publicly disown his right as his heir before the Bishop. Francis stripping himself of even the clothes he was wearing which was bought by his father, Pietro Bernardone, firmly declared, *"Pietro Bernardone is no longer my father. From now on I can say with complete freedom, 'Our Father who art in heaven...'"* From there Francis walked out into the world without anything from his earthly father but gaining everything from his Father in heaven. St. Francis' spiritual journey thus started.

Francis felt he heard a voice from Jesus to rebuild His Church, which at that time was fraught with scandal, avarice and many heresies. He set out without anything to do this. His deep prayerful life, exemplary compassion and preaching won him companions. Soon, a cream of friars of Francis was formed. These friars formed a unique brotherhood, based on pure love of God and sharing in the Gospel values together. They lived on arms and went in pairs preaching on bare foot. The spirit of Francis was so contagious that this brotherhood included nature and animals. He was at home with woods, flowers, trees, birds and animals. He preached to all with his life about the goodness of God. In fact, the friars reported how much Francis sees God in everything around him; as they said, he is so taken up in contemplating and seeing God in everything later in his life that when he is at the table with his friars, he no longer knows the difference between the taste of wine and water. Life has no taste outside God for Francis.

When St. Francis was forty years, in 1224, he made a pilgrimage to a Mountain (La Verna), for a special prayer and fasting he calls the "Lent of St. Michael" (from August 15 – the Solemnity of Assumption – to September 29, the feast of Archangel Michael). Francis spent long time on the Mountain meditating on the Passion of Christ. His life request to Jesus, as one he passionately loves, had been to grant him the favour of sharing in his passion by feeling his wounds in his own body. Barely thirty days into his prayer and fasting, on the 14th day of September, feast of the Exultation of the Cross, Francis was visited by a Seraph from heaven. Bob and Penny chronicled the experience thus:

> *A figure came forth, slowly, and carried the brilliant light with it.*
> *Francis couldn't look at it; the light was too strong. Then the Lord*

allowed Francis' eyes to open. Before him, suspended in the air, was a huge Angel, who appeared to be made of fire, he was so bright; but there were no flames coming from him. He had six wings, two extended over his head, two extended as if for flight, and two covering his body. The Angel was nailed to a cross; the wounds of Jesus flared up, and shivered against the light. They were of a deep crimson, sprinkled with gold. Francis stood up joyfully, to greet the Seraph. At that moment, beams of heated illumination shot out of the Angel's wounds, and penetrated Francis' body, hands, feet and side. He fell from the force of the thrust; his body experienced devastating pain, mixed with inconceivable joy. His blood raced throughout his body; he was sure he would die. Then the sensation calmed down to a constant throb of joy and pain. He looked up at the Heavenly Creature. The eyes of the Angel were studying Francis. The stare was compelling. There was at once fear and bliss, mixed together...the eyes of the Angel were the most beautiful he had ever seen. He could not look away from them. The heavenly vision spoke gently to Francis' heart. He told him things he had to hear, which were for him alone; he would not in his lifetime, reveal them to anyone. He stayed with Francis for the better part of an hour. This is according to the testimony of the farmers, and mule keepers at the foot of the mountain. They mistook the brilliant light for the sun coming up, and began their day. Then, when it disappeared, and the natural sun came out, it was colourless by comparison.[182]

The encounter St. Francis had with the Seraph confirms again a number of issues we have earlier presented about the Angels:

1. That the *Seraphim* are the flame of God.
2. Biblically they are Angels with six wings (Is. 6:2).

---

[182] B., & P. LORD, *Angels in the Lives of the Saints*, electronic ibook, pp. 85-90.

3. They are the purest fire, colourfully more beautiful than any earthly creature or colour. Their brilliance is nothing to be compared with the sun.

It is not just Bob and Penny's description, the first biographer of St. Francis, Thomas of Celano, in his own account, simply said that the Seraph's beauty was "indescribable".[183] Those living around –the farmers and mule keepers – the mountain of La Verna saw the brilliant light from the encounter of St. Francis with the Angel and thought the sun has risen. That means it was an experience described by more than one person. All still supports our study that Angels are real Messengers of God.

2.2   St. Thomas of Aquino

In 1225 AD, when a boy was to born to Landulph, the Count of Aquino, nobody knew that someone with cherubic intelligence was born in Lombardy of Naples in Italy. Thomas came last of eight siblings born of the same mother, Theodora, the Countess of Teano. Belonging to the family of Nobles, at the age of five, Thomas was sent to Monte Cassino to be educated by the Benedictine Monks. From the early stage of his life, he was very sharp intellectually and was already constantly questioning the Monks: "What is God?" The family had hopes from the way he was manifesting his intelligence early that one day he will be the Abbot of the famous Benedictine Monastery in Monte Cassino.

But political turmoil of that time forced Thomas at the age of thirteen to come back to Naples and continue his education in a Benedictine house there affiliated to the University of Naples. He later studied in the University of Naples, picking particular interest in the Philosophy of Aristotle. While there, Thomas developed new interest with the Friars of St. Dominic and privately accepted their habit. His family wanted him to return to the family loyalty to the Benedictine shrine of Monte Cassino. They considered his flip to the Dominicans as betrayal. Her mother set out in search of him to bring him home to get him back to his senses. When it was not easy to make Thomas change his decision, the family forcefully abducted him from the Dominicans and kept him under "house-arrest" in a Castle, the fortress of San Giovani at Rocca

---

[183] "Medieval Sourcebook: Thomas of Celano: Lives of St. Francis". Online article: www.Fordham.edu. Accessed 15-08-2012.

Secca. Thomas remained for a year as a prisoner in this castle prison and still refused to be changed. The brothers decided to incarcerate his spiritual strength by introducing a seductive woman into his room. When Thomas realized their intention, he made a sword out of a glowing wood from the fire and pursued the woman out of the room. Thereafter, Thomas earnestly prayed for the strength to overcome their evil plots for him.

When Thomas fell asleep, he saw a vision of Angels who came to him and tied around his waste a heavenly *chord of chastity*. Strengthened by this, Thomas for the rest of his life was able to withstand all lustful seductions to spiritual and material impurity. This kept him pure in mind and spirit; helping his intellect to reach deep into the mysteries of God, especially later in his academic life as a Philosopher and Theologian.

He later studied in Cologne under St. Albert the Great between 1248 and 1252. He was observed to be a very quiet student but very sharp in presenting either his thesis or objecting to a thesis. Fellow students nicknamed him *the Dumb-Ox*. St. Albert who noticed what was in Thomas was quoted to have said to the students once in his comment: "You call him 'the Dumb Ox,' but one day the bellowing of this Ox will resound throughout the world". The prophecy of this holy Teacher evidently came true. Today, St. Thomas Aquinas is known among all the holy Doctors of the Church as the *Angelic Doctor*. This name was given to him for two obvious reasons: He has a *Cherubic* physique – very deep and sober personality and no one has written on the nature, existence and ministries of Angels like him. This special credit is given to him for his lofty contributions in exposing the deep things of God through his theology, but particularly because he discussed the Holy Angels with consistent logic from the Scriptures. St. Thomas clearly leads us to understand that no normal human mind can go beyond the sensible abstractions to pierce the mysteries of God unless he is helped by the illumination that comes from the Holy Angels whom he calls "pure intelligences". He writes for example,

> Hence Angels propose the intelligible truth to men under the
> likeness of sensible things and strengthen the human mind by an
> intellectual operation. In this twofold action consists angelic
> illumination of men. By adding to the human understanding to
> pierce the mysteries of being, the pure intelligences enable it to

derive greater truth from the species abstracted from sensible things. Thus men rise with angelic assistance to a more perfect knowledge of God drawn from a knowledge of his creation[184]

My interest in presenting St. Thomas is not to teach his doctrines but to show how far those who are accompanied by the Angels can reach their height. Of course, we do not need to argue again if his special Angel is from the Cherubim. No other choir of Angels can illuminate the human mind for deep theology or philosophy or even other scientific knowledge of nature, of the spheres, and of God, like the Cherubim. But we need to realize from Thomas' life history that through his dogged effort, he fought off the corruption of lust and seduction. He prayed down on himself the gift of chastity which now gave these pure Angels free access to his body, mind and spirit to operate, illuminating him with wonderful things of God. How else could he have written the *"Lauda Sion Salvatorem"* on the Eucharist? Could normal human mind on its own write it? We really need the Angels for good knowledge. If you are a student, a Lecturer, Professor or someone involved with any literate venture or academic carrier, you need the Angels to help your ailing brains. Even if you are not in anyway academic, to read and understand well the Scriptures, spiritual writings and holy speeches or sermons, you need the assistance of these Angels. Through their light, our poor carnal minds could be elevated to receive from high frequency of divine revelations.

2.3   St. Frances of Rome

Santa Francesca Romana (St. Frances of Rome) was born (1384) almost two centuries after her countryman, St. Francis of Assisi. Unlike Francis, she knew what God wanted of her early. At the age of 11years, she was already very pious and had decided to enter into the monastery to live as a religious, but her Father gave her into marriage with Lorenzo Ponziani, the son of a fellow Roman Noble when she was only 13 years old. However, her husband Lorenzo loved and cared so much for her. Her only torture in the family was that she was exposed to live as nobles, receiving and entertaining visitors in parties and revelry. Her mother in-law was greatly at odds with her in this area for she loved to party. Frances, gradually got the consolation and company of her sister in-law, Vannozza, from whom she learnt to gladly attend to her family duties first and then steal out to pray and do charity. Frances was dedicated to her prayers and

---

[184] *Summa Theologiae*, Ia, 51, 2 ad 1.

charity. She had the gift of miracles from God on many occasions concerning her family and life of charity.

On one occasion, Frances' Father-in-law sold off the excess grains in their house because he thought that Frances was giving too much to the poor. He believed that leaving just enough for the family will stop the pious Frances from practicing her commitment to the poor. She took to begging to continue her care for the poor. One day, in desperation to have something for the poor, she searched the now empty granary loft of the family for a possible kernel left with corn. When she left, her husband Lorenzo found that the family reserve has been miraculously refilled with corn and wine. This incident converted the Father-in-law and Lorenzo to allow Frances practice her charity freely.

Another instance of her miraculous favours from God occurred when civil war raged among the nobles and the ruling parties, including the Pope and the anti-popes in Rome. As the result of the feud, Frances' first son, Battista, was to be taken as a hostage to stop the Ponziani family from participating in the war. She attempted to flee with her son, but through the counsel of her Spiritual Director, Don Andrew, she resorted to prayer for God's will to be done. Frances stayed in the Church crying to God about her son. When the soldiers came to take Battista, none of the horses they put him could move. The soldiers left the boy and he ran to her mother praying in the Church and embraced her.

Although Frances saved Battista her first son from the soldiers, the plague that struck Rome in 1411 claimed the life of her second son Evangelista. The holy woman did not give up on her prayers and charity. Evangelista, a year after his death, visited her mother, Frances, while she was praying. In the vision, Frances saw Evangelista brilliant in the company of another more brilliant boy. He told her mother that he came to console her; she should not worry because her little sister Agnes will soon join them in Heaven. He assured her that God is now granting her the gift of an Archangel to be her special Guardian and director. She would have the privilege of seeing him and taking instructions from him till her death.

From that vision, Frances always sees the special Guardian from Heaven besides her. Agnes died a year later as she was told. Frances described the Angel to have the appearance of a little boy less than ten years. His face shines with compassion and kindness. With the radiance from his presence, Frances could read her office. The heavenly Guard followed her wherever she went walking either before or besides her, helping to discern the people she met, their evil or good intentions and scaring away the evil forces attempting to attack her. When Frances husband, Lorenzo died and was buried beside her two sons, Frances now fully joined the group of women she had formed as Oblates of Mary for works of charity. It was narrated that on the particular day she was eventually freed from her family duty to realize her childhood dreams of living alone for God, she was given a vision of Jesus seating on His throne with countless number of Angels surrounding and worshipping Him. She then saw a new Angel from the rank of Powers appointed by the Lord to replace the Archangel who had been her guard. This Angel remained with her the remaining four years of her life. Frances noted the presence of this Angel scared away any fallen Angel from her. The Lord granted her a lot of vision, both of heaven and of hell. When it was time for her to die, she smiled to her companions who stood around her bed and said, "The Angel has finished his task. He beckons me to follow him." She attracted a lot of companions more in death than when she was alive. Oblates of Mary still exist, clothing themselves like noble ladies of the era of St. Frances. She was canonized in 1608 by Pope Paul V, and 9th of March was assigned as her feast day.

From this holy woman, we have another confirmation of how much closer the Angels stay to us. Not only do we have them for a guard, God often assigns a special Angel for someone who has been chosen for a special work as we saw in Frances' case. When someone undertakes a special work for love of God and neighbour, God assigns to the person Angels adapted for those area of work. Our Guardian Angels can be from any rank, depending on the mission one is involved. Everyone needs to realize why God sent him into the world. What mission he has been called to do. How much you are into it will help to discern the presence of these heavenly co-workers and Messengers of God. Angels are really closer to us than the demons we fear. I believe that when one neither feels the presence of these heavenly helpers nor the scourge of fallen Angels, he has been grounded or zeroed to a halt in spiritual life. The enemy makes him believe that neither exists so that he may not struggle to start moving again. This situation is more serious than those scared of seeing the devil everywhere.

2.4   Don Bosco and the Gray One (*il Grigio*)

Don Giovani Melchior Bosco was born in August 16, 1815 when the Napoleonic wars and great famine was wrecking the foot mountain countryside of Becchi, in Italy. His father, Francesco Bosco died when he was only two, leaving the mother, Margaret, with the care of Giovani and his two elder brothers, Antonio and Giuseppe. Her mother influenced him at the early stage of his life to work hard, behave well, and pray even while working in the farm.

At the age of nine (1825), Giovani wrote in his memoirs that, while sleeping one night, he dreamt of seeing a huge numbers of poor boys playing and blaspheming. These boys were rude and ill behaved. Then, he saw in the dream a man well dressed and with magnificent appearance who said to him, "*You will have to win these friends of yours not with blows, but with gentleness and kindness. So begin right now to show them that sin is ugly and virtue beautiful*", then a Lady also magnificently dressed, added "*Make yourself humble, strong and robust. At the right time you will understand everything*". This dream left on Giovani a lasting impression though he did not understand yet they were referring to his calling.

Five years later (1830), overcoming the odds of poverty and determined to pursue his heart yearning, Giovani left for seminary through the help and support of an elderly good Priest, Don Cafasso. After 11 years of training (On June 5, 1841), the Archbishop of Turin ordained Giovani Bosco a Priest and he was popularly called Don Bosco. He made himself available to help the young boys because he still remembered his childhood dream. With much dedication and perseverance, he overcame many obstacles and opened up an *oratorio* (named after St. Francis de Sales) to help these boys he picks up from the streets. The rest of forty-seven years of Don Bosco's pastoral work was dedicated to these youth. My attention is drawn to the particular incidents that occurred in his pastoral life with the *GRAY ONE, (IL GRIGIO).*

The work Don Bosco was doing among the delinquent boys was not appreciated by a lot of people for different reasons. His life was threatened several times. He had no arms to protect himself but that did not stop him from carrying on the job. He trusted in the watchful eyes of the One who called him to this vocation. I will only recount three incidents out of those recorded in Don Bosco's memoir regarding his friend, *il Grigio.*

Don Bosco was returning home late one evening in 1852 along *Piazza Emanuele Filiberto*. Suddenly, he realized that someone was coming after him with a club in his hands. He started to run hoping to reach home before the assailant could get him. Before he could reach *Via Cottolengo*, the road that joins to the *Oratorio*, he saw several others across the road, with clubs coming after him too. Finding himself in the midst of them, he stopped running to face the single one behind him. He strongly elbowed him before he could hit him and the poor wretch fell to ground crying, "I am dead! I am dead!" The others surrounded him. He realized that he was in a great danger. But just at that instant, behold a huge fierce looking "Gray *(Grigio)*" Mastiff dog from nowhere jumped to his side growling and howling dangerously to his assailants. The Scoundrels were all paralyzed with fear and they begged Don Bosco to hold the dog from tearing at them. Don Bosco made them promise they will not attack anybody in the streets again. They ran off and *il Grigio* did not go after them but walked Don Bosco to his door and disappeared.

Another incident happened in December 1854. He was returning late on a dark and foggy night. He was descending from Via *Consolata* towards Via *Cottolengo*. He turned and spotted two men following him with some distance. They increased their pace if he quickens up his own and slows with him too. He was then sure they were after him. Before he could do anything more the men came upon, throwing a cloak over his head. He managed to free his head from the cloak attempting to shout for help but they stuck his mouth with a handkerchief. Just at that moment, *il Grigio* came bouncing upon them with the roaring of a hungry wolf, kicking them off to the mud. The dog then stopped by the side of Don Bosco growling at the two men with a threat to tear them if they make further movement towards the Priest. They again begged Don Bosco to save their lives from the dog, apologizing and asking him to forgive them. The dog walked Don Bosco home and disappeared.

The last instance we would like to recount is a case where *il Grigio* prevented Don Bosco from leaving the house. It happened that Don Bosco had a call to attend at night. Her mother Margaret advised him not to leave the house because it was late and dangerous, but he convinced her not to be afraid. Reaching the entrance gate, he saw *il Grigio* lying in front of the gate. He exclaimed, "Behold, *il Grigio*! Much better, we have a good company, rise up and follow me". But the dog growled menacingly at him and refused to rise up. One of the boys with Don Bosco touched the dog with his leg to get him up but the dog growled fiercely at him. Mamma Margaret who was still worried came upon them and said to his son, "if you will not listen to me, listen at least to the dog's warning, and do not go out. Don Bosco turned back with the boys. At that moment, someone ran up to him panting and breathless asking him not to attempt leaving the house that night because four armed men are roaming the street determined to kill him. Don Bosco realized that again, *il Grigio* appeared to save his life. Don Bosco dedicated the last chapter of his memoir to this strange dog he calls "*il Grigio*".

The question he strangely never answered was who was this *Grigio*, and from where does he appear. He never really made a big show of the dog. But this dog stayed around him for over thirty years protecting him and reassuring him at every needed moment that he was safe with him around. The last entry Don Bosco made in his memoir of the *il Grigio* was in 1866, but a friend recounted that Don Bosco told him that the dog still accompanied him in 1883 to Ventimiglia, a road along the Italian boarders with the French. When the friend dared to ask Don Bosco if dogs could live that long, he laughingly replied that it could the son or the grandson of *il Grigio*. Later, after Don Bosco had long died, some Salesians have occasionally witnessed the protection of *il Grigio* between 1893 and 1930. What sort dog spanned 80 years of protection to the Founder and the Salesians? Don Bosco himself was once quoted to have said, "It sounds ridiculous to call him an Angel, yet he is no ordinary dog…" If the dog is not an Angel, who do you think he is?

2.5   St. Gemma of Galgani

In Gemma, we are telling the story of a Saint that lived two centuries ago. Like the rest of the Saints in our story, she was Italian too.

St. Gemma Galgani

Gemma was born towards the end of 19th century, on March 12, 1878, named Maria Gemma Umberta Pia Galgani. She was born at Borgo Nuovo, countryside near Lucca in the Province of Capannori. Her Father, Enrico Galgani was a prosperous Pharmacist and her mother, Aurelia died when Gemma was still seven years old.

To get better education, they transferred to the city of Lucca in Tuscana Province. She received her first communion when she was 9 years old and everyone could see her piety and love of prayers from her early years. Gemma schooled at a Catholic School run by Sisters of St. Zita. She was very intelligent and reserved at school and was loved by many, although she was always sickly. Her sickness could not allow her to continue her education. Her father died also when she was completing her 18th year, leaving her with the family responsibility of caring for the other siblings. Her aunt, Carolina, assisted her greatly. She later became a housekeeper with an adopted family, the Gianinni.

Gemma wanted to join the Passionist convent but she was not admitted because of her poor health. She declined suitors, and with the help of her confessor, advanced so much in her hunger to keep herself for Christ. In all the neighbourhood of Lucca, she was well known and admired for her virtues. Some called her "the Virgin of Lucca". She also suffered a lot of ridicule from many who thought she was mental because of her extraordinary mystical experiences. However, she died at the age of 25 (April 11, 1903) and was canonized 37 years (1940) after her death.

It would be good to narrate some of Gemma's experiences with her Guardian Angel. She is one of those Saints in the Catholic Church that was gifted with prolonged interaction with her Guardian Angel. As one of her chronicler and Spiritual Director, Venerable Fr. Germano, summarized it,

> *Gemma saw her guardian angel with her own eyes, touched him with her hand, as if he were a being of this world, and would talk to him as would one friend to another.*
>
> *"Jesus" she once said "has not left me alone; He makes my guardian angel stay with me always".*

God does not give extraordinary spiritual gifts in vain. Gemma was selected as a *Victim Soul*; someone who will through penance and sacrifices purify herself and many souls for Christ. That was why she had to suffer many things from family deaths and misfortunes to personal humiliations of ill health, academic dropout, and rejection from the Passionists' religious house she had desperately wanted. The things Gemma suffered would have been attributed to "ancestral issues" to be dealt with through cleansing prayer and rituals if suffered by a present day devoted Christian in our area (Nigeria). One would think Gemma would not have understood it herself if she did not receive the favour of seeing her Guardian Angel.

The presence and companionship of her lovely friend and Angel made her steadfast and fervent in prayers. Gemma's holy Spiritual Director, Venerable Germano di Stanislao, wrote a biography of her spiritual daughter after her death in a book (*The Life of St. Gemma Galgani*), recounting what Gemma had told him; he described the companionship between Gemma and her Guardian Angel with regards to prayer:

> *...He let her see him sometimes raised in the air with outspread wings, with his hands extended over her, or else hands joined in an attitude of prayer. At other times he would kneel beside her. If they were reciting vocal prayers or the Psalms, they did so alternately; if aspirations or prayers from the heart, "they rivaled one another" [these are Gemma's words] that is, they had a holy rivalry as to whom would say them with more fervor saying 'Viva Gesu' or 'Benedetto di Dio' and other such beautiful invocations. When it was time for meditation, the angel inspired her with sublimest ideas, and moved her affections so that the result of this holy exercise may be more perfect. The subject of these meditations was, for the most part, the Passion of Our Lord, the angel like a good master, laid open its profound mysteries to her soul. "Look" he would exclaim, "at what Jesus suffered for men. Consider each of these wounds. It is love that has opened them all, See how horrible sin is, since to expiate it, so much pain and so much love have been necessary"*

There is no doubt that Gemma, who experienced the extraordinary hand of God in her life, was always ready to give more of herself for love of God. Think of the blissful moments you experience when you accomplish a difficult feat even in the material world. For instance, you are named the best in the class after tedious and sleepless nights of studies, or, you top the bests in any sports or commercial competition out of serious hard work not merit. To win such competitions takes much physical and psychological toll on the competitors. But they are glad always to go through them provided at the end they have the crown (cf. 1 Cor 9:24-27). The same with Gemma and *Victims for Souls*; they have already seen the prize awaiting their sufferings, and they gladly embrace it for the pleasure of the Spouse and Reward, Jesus. How could she had sustained her weak and mortal body continuously in the pleasures of heavenly things for long if her Angel and other mystical experiences she was having were not granted to her? Even with those experiences, she still struggled with the flesh as she wrote in her autobiography:

> One evening, when I was suffering more than usual, I was complaining to Jesus and telling him that I would not have prayed so much if I had known that He was not going to cure me, and I asked Him why I had to be sick this way. My angel answered me as follows: 'If Jesus afflicts you in your body, it is always to purify you in your soul. Be good.' Oh, how many times during my long illness did I not experience such consoling words in my heart! But I never profited by them."

If Gemma, who talked with the Holy Ones, had difficulty enduring physical suffering, how much could one who do not believe in holy realities endure it? The presence of this Holy Messenger whose consolation succored her pains helped Gemma to persevere to the crown of being remembered today as a Saint, a Holy One.

Gemma's Guardian Angel was there always to *guide* her, *reprove* her, and *instruct* her. She acknowledged that without the presence of her Guardian, she would have been into a lot of mess:

> He corrected me every time I did something wrong, and he taught me to speak but little, and only when I was spoken to. One day, when those in the house were speaking of some person, and were not speaking very well of her, I wanted to speak up, but the angel gave me a severe rebuke. He taught me to keep my eyes cast down, and one time in Church he reproved me strongly saying to me 'Is this the way you conduct yourself in the presence of God?'

She also remembered that even when she was trying to persevere with all these, the Holy Guardian reminds her of how imperfect she still was by saying to her; *"Poor child! How imperfect you are! How much you need others to keep a constant guard over thee. Oh, how much patience I must have with thee"*. In spite of these rebuke, the Angel was her best lover and one who took care of her the most. Gemma truly understood from the Angel that the way God approaches worldly things is quite different from the way we (human beings) approach it. She recounted one day when she wore a new golden watch given to her out and came back happy, the Angel told her to always remember, *"The precious jewelry that adorns the spouse of the Crucified King can only be thorns and the cross"*. How could one quench the burning carnal cravings for material well being unless some intervention of divine grace visits us from above? More so, if it visits us tangibly in the personal love, care and direction our Guardian Angels like Gemma's. It is sincere and ardent love in our soul that will provoke God to visit us as He did to Gemma, although in a manner peculiar to our respective callings. Gemma loved Jesus Christ so much from her earliest years, and much more later as she passed through her pains and ecstasies. This love was transferred to her Guardian Angel too as Fr. Germano observed: *"Gemma, seeing the great charity her angel lavished upon her, loved her angel immensely, and his name was always on her tongue as well as in her heart." 'Dear Angel' she would say 'I love you so!' 'And why' the Angel asked. 'Because you teach me how to be good, and to keep humble, and to please Jesus'."*

Looking at the companionship between Gemma and her Guardian Angel would make one wish that his or her own Guardian Angel would appear also to him or her. But let us remember, as Gemma told her Angel, "I love you most because you make me to be good, you make me to be humble and to please Jesus". It is the last reason, 'to please Jesus', which was the uppermost desire of her life that made Jesus to give her the gift of one who will help her know the best way to please him. If anyone wants to see his or her Guardian Angel, what would be the uppermost reason for that? Anyway, that would not be possible until the day God's mercies grant that person the grace to be always ready to obey the Angel like St. Gemma, seing the Angel with the physical eye is a special grace. A believer would always want his or her Angels to stay around doing their heavenly duties over him or her without physically seeing him. It is a joy to know that the Angels are there for us, especially every time the material world is blurring our vision of our homeland, heaven.

2.6 Padre Pio di Pietrelcina

From Gemma of Galgani, we move down to San Giovani Rotondo in the Province of Foggia, southern Italy for the last Saint we will sample in our effort to show that the biblical facts we presented in this study were actually lived out by some people we know. This last Saint lived in our own era towards the close of 20th century, and could be the contemporary of many people, St. *Padre Pio di Pietrelcina.*

Padre Pio di Pietrelcina.

Pietrelcina is a little country town in the Province of Benevento, located south of Italy. There on May 25, 1887, Maria Guiseppa Forgione gave birth to a son, whom his father Grazio Mario Forgione named Francesco, after his late brother who he lost very early. The piety of this boy began early because, at the age of five years, he had already decided to set himself apart for Jesus. He served as an altar boy at the town Chapel located on the Castle hill. Her mother, spotted Francesco even as little as he was, inflicting penance on himself, like sleeping on the floor and using pebbles on his pillow. Her mother testified that she noticed the boy could see and talk with Jesus, Mary and his Guardian Angel. Conversing with him, Francesco thought that every other child could do the same.

The Capuchin Friars received Francesco as a novice at the age of 15 (Jan. 6, 1903) clothing him with the much-desired habit of St. Francis. He took the name of the Patron Saint of Pietrelcina, Pio. He took his solemn profession on January 1907 and was ordained Padre Pio three years after in 1910 at the Cathedral of Benevento. He celebrated his first mass at the Church of Our Lady of the Angels. He lived and served in Our Lady of Grace Capuchin Friary in San Giovani Rotondo almost all his life. Though when the First World War broke out, he was called briefly to military service (1917), which lasted for only 182 days. He returned to San Giovani Rotondo where his popularity in spiritual matters attracted to him a lot of spiritual sons and daughters. He attended to a lot of people seeking spiritual help. His rule for growth in spiritual journey for all his wards were:

1. *Weekly Confessions* – which he likened to sweeping of your room every week.
2. *Daily Communion* – feed oneself with strength from above to withstand the evil one and not be famished with worldliness.
3. *Spiritual Reading* – giving your mind and spirit the raw material helpful for meditation and continuous contemplation of God's goodness.
4. *Meditation* – dwelling on divine goodness and willing to do his bidding always.
5. *Examination of Conscience* – returning to the God every morning before one begins the day and every evening in retrospection of how the day was spent.

All his life Padre Pio believed that to love God is to be ready to suffer everything for His sake. He experienced a lot of soldiers dying unprepared during his short military service during the war. He was willing to accept more suffering from the Lord because of his vision of lost souls and suffering souls (he was quoted to have said 'more numbers of suffering souls attend his masses than the living congregation'). Since Pope Benedict XV appealed to Christian to pray for the end of the First World War, which was ravaging lives in Europe, Padre Pio offered himself privately to God as a *"Victim for the end of the War"*. In answer to his offering, he received the piercing of his heart with the lance of love from the Lord – *transverberation* – as a mark that his heart and the heart of Jesus are united in sufferings for love of souls. Padre Pio wrote to his Spiritual Director, Padre Benedetto narrating his experience thus:

> *While I was hearing the boys' confessions on the evening of the 5th [August] I was suddenly terrorized by the sight of a celestial person who presented himself to my mind's eye. He had in his hand a sort of weapon like a very long sharp-pointed steel blade which seemed to emit fire. At the very instant that I saw all this, I saw that person hurl the weapon into my soul with all his might. I cried out with difficulty and felt I was dying. I asked the boy to leave because I felt ill and no longer had the strength to continue. This agony lasted uninterruptedly until the morning of the 7th. I cannot tell you how much I suffered during this period of anguish.*

> *Even my entrails were torn and ruptured by the weapon, and*
> *nothing was spared. From that day on I have been mortally*
> *wounded. I feel in the depths of my soul a wound that is always*
> *open and which causes me continual agony.*

This occurred in August 5, 1918. He was sustaining the wound and the pains when the same 'celestial person' visited him again on the choir loft of the Church where he was praying before a crucifix. This time, the visitor left him with permanent scares of the whole wounds of Jesus, which he had to suffer for the rest of his life. Padre Pio, on a letter written a month after the experience (October 22, 1918) to his Director, tells his story:

> *On the morning of the 20th of last month, in the choir, after I had*
> *celebrated Mass I yielded to a drowsiness similar to a sweet sleep.*
> *[...] I saw before me a mysterious person similar to the one I had*
> *seen on the evening of 5 August. The only difference was that his*
> *hands and feet and side were dripping blood. This sight terrified me*
> *and what I felt at that moment is indescribable. I thought I should*
> *have died if the Lord had not intervened and strengthened my heart*
> *which was about to burst out of my chest. The vision disappeared*
> *and I became aware that my hands, feet and side were dripping*
> *blood. Imagine the agony I experienced and continue to experience*
> *almost every day. The heart wound bleeds continually, especially*
> *from Thursday evening until Saturday. Dear Father, I am dying of*
> *pain because of the wounds and the resulting embarrassment I feel*
> *deep in my soul. I am afraid I shall bleed to death if the Lord does*
> *not hear my heartfelt supplication to relieve me of this condition.*
> *Will Jesus, who is so good, grant me this grace? Will he at least*
> *free me from the embarrassment caused by these outward signs? I*
> *will raise my voice and will not stop imploring him until in his*
> *mercy he takes away, not the wound or the pain, which is*
> *impossible since I wish to be inebriated with pain, but these*

outward signs which cause me such embarrassment and unbearable humiliation.

We have given above the full quotation of Padre Pio's story because it is very unusual to find someone who offers himself to be a victim to suffer for others, to obtain divine graces for many who have not even asked for it let alone acknowledging the effort. We know that it is very rare to find someone under continuous excruciating pain and suffering who will be praying not to have the pain and suffering removed but only to hide it from the sight of people. People shout and clamour for others to see the little sacrifices or pains they bear for them. They would want them to acknowledge it and thank the Lord (although I mean myself here) for it. Here is a man completely different. Padre Pio was an extraordinary victim for souls. For this, he experienced celestial visitors (holy and unholy ones) and was granted extraordinary favour with the Holy Angels. We will cite just few instances of his activities with his Guardian Angel he fondly called *Angelino*.

From his childhood, Padre Pio related with his Guardian Angels like a family sibling. Only that this particular family member is different and special to him than other members of the family in everything. He shared everything with his Angel and relied on him for everything. The Angel is never tired of him and was always loving and caring in spite of Padre Pio's behaviours sometimes. In a letter, Padre Pio wrote to one of his spiritual daughters, counseling her to take her own Guardian Angel serious and treat him as one of the loved members of her family. This is the way it should be because that is how he (P. Pio) treats his own. He wrote:

> *"Oh, Raffaelina, where do my thoughts fly to now...? Treat this dear little Angel, I do not say as a friend, but as one of the family. And, to tell you the truth, this little Angel does not seem to be the least little bit offended by my treatment of him. How dear and how good he is"* (cf. Letters vol. II, no. 64).

What could Padre Pio have done without his *Angelino* (*little Angel*)? He depended on him for practically everything. To give an example, when Padre was getting weaker, he had a helper, Fr. Alessio Parente (who has written so much of these accounts as eye witness). Fr Alessio was supposed to stand by as P. Pio finishes the Mass every day to help him pass through the surging pilgrims to his cell. Fr. Alessio recounted that he always over slept. Sometimes, the alarm clock fails or sometimes he must have put the alarm clock off and continued sleeping. But he realized that each time he over slept, he would hear a voice knocking on his door and calling out to him; "Alessio, Alessio come down!". When he jumps out of the bed and gets to the door, he would find nobody there. Alessio found out who the caller was the day he attempted to excuse himself for his lateness to Padre Pio. He wrote,

> One day I was sitting by Padre Pio's side, feeling ashamed at my lack of punctuality. I was trying to explain to him that I never seemed to hear the alarm, but he interrupted me. 'Yes, I understand you,' he said. 'But do you think I will continue to send my guardian angel every day to wake you? You'd better go and buy yourself a new clock.' It was only then that I realized who was knocking at my door and calling me in my sleep.

Yes! Fr. Alessio needed a new clock instead of befriending and relying on his own Guardian Angel to wake him up to his daily duties. Padre Pio, older, weaker, over burdened and suffering more has no need of alarm clock but a younger, stronger and less burdened Fr. Alessio needed one. People usually needs alarm clock to wake them up. But for those who believe and trust in these *Holy Celestial Friends*, things could be different. That is what Padre Pio was teaching Alessio.

There were eyewitnesses who were marveled by how Padre Pio could speak and read foreign languages without studying them. When asked how he could do that, he simply said that his *Angelino* knows all languages. Take the example narrated in Fr. Alessio' s account in the book, *Send me Your Guardian Angel*:

> A little American girl was brought to Padre Pio so that he could hear her first confession. Since she didn't speak a word of Italian, an American religious sister by the name of Mary Pyle, who was close to Father Pio, brought the little girl to him. 'Father, I'm here to help you as this little girl doesn't understand any Italian at all.'

> *"'Mary,' said Padre Pio, 'you can go, as the little one and I will take care of this.' Mary Pyle waited outside and when the little girl emerged from confession, she asked her, 'Did Padre Pio understand you?' 'Yes,' came the reply. Mary, a little surprised, asked one more question: 'Did he speak in English?' 'Yes, in English,' said the little girl."*

That is certainly exceptional gift that may not be repeated every day. But it shows that Angels are real, and with them, we can do many things other than speaking foreign languages. Or at least, they could help one to learn the foreign language faster and easily.

If one has the chance to read the three volumes of the compilation of the Letters of Padre Pio, one will be marveled by how much he used his *Angelino* to attend to numerous clients. We will give only three stories of Padre Pio and his curia Angel.

1.   STORY 1 – *The Angel Driver*

An Italian Lawyer, who frequented San Giovani Rotondo to attend Masses of Padre Pio, was returning home with his family (wife and two sons). He grew drowsy on the steering because of long driving. Before he could stop to rest a while, he fell asleep on the steering and he could not tell the rest of the story except that when the car eventually stopped, he woke up asking the family what happened. The wife and children were astonished when they saw how the car ran off the right track and was being expertly controlled against hitting the on coming vehicles and falling into a ditch. The man realized from where they were that he slept for fifteen kilometers. The whole family was astonished at the miracle. When few months later the Lawyer visited San Giovani Rotondo, Padre Pio said to him as soon as he saw him, "You slept and the Guardian Angel drove your car." He realized who saved the family and was grateful for that heavenly intervention.

2.   STORY 2 – *Curia Angels*

Fr. Alessio recounted how he went one day to consult Padre Pio with some urgent messages he had from mails. When he approached the saintly man to confer with him, he told him abruptly, "Don't you see that I am busy? Leave me alone." Fr. Alessio left him. Later, Padre Pio called Fr. Alessio and said to him, *"Have you seen all those angels that were near me? They were the Guardian Angels of my spiritual children that came to bring me their messages. I had to report to them the answers they needed."* Where as many sort their mails in the post office, this holy man simply maximized God given gift of the Holy Messengers. It is wonderful to see what gift we have in these Holy Guardians.

3.   STOR Y 3 – *An Angel to heal…*

An Italian girl heard stories of how Padre Pio uses Angels to help many people. When his uncle Fred was very ill and she was afraid he would not recover; she prayed to her guardian Angel to go to Padre Pio to solicit for healing on behalf of his uncle. The uncle recovered. When the girl visited Padre Pio to thank him, immediately Padre Pio saw her, he said to her: "Your Angel kept me up all night, asking for a cure for your uncle Fred." The girl was very happy that her Angel actually responded to her request.

Another story was told of a woman whose child was mortally ill. In desperation, she invoked the child's Guardian Angel to go to Padre Pio for intervention in the little baby's case. Soon after she made this mental invocation, the little baby reacted positively as if pricked by something. Her health immediately improved and she was discharged from the intensive care unit. The doctors were surprised at such quick recovery.

2.7   Lessons from the Testimonies of Saints

To conclude this section of our study, we would like to present to the reader a few lessons for further reflection and contemplation. These lessons witness to the reality and goodness of the Angels as God's eternal help to man.

First, from the testimonies of the Hebrew Testament, Christian Apostolic Testament, Patristic Testament and finally the testimonies of Saints spanning from the earliest Middle Ages to our contemporary times, Angels have been evidently shown to exist, co-habit and serve human beings at the bidding of God. Their service to human being is not imaginary. The lives of the six Italian Saints we sampled, among many others, indicate how close and available God has destined them to us. THUS, THROUGHOUT HISTORY, ANGELS BELIEVE IN MEN, BUT DO MEN BELIEVE IN THE HOLY ANGELS OF GOD?

Second, from the enormous witness of the Holy Scriptures cited in this study and many other works on the Angels and from the records of the eyewitnesses cited here and elsewhere, could all these be mythical or fables made up along the ages and still continued in our times as some modernist thinking suggests? With the life of such practical Saint like Padre Pio of Pietrelcina, it would be ridiculous to continue believing that these Holy Beings are not real. TO THE ANGELS, HUMAN BEINGS ARE NOT FAIRY STORY, BUT TO SOME HUMAN BEINGS, ANGELS ARE FAIRY STORY.

Third, one could easily notice from the lives of the Saints above, and similar people chosen who were granted the favour to see their Angels with their physical eyes, that they were in one way or the other connected with suffering in a special way. They mostly shared in the passion of Jesus Christ crucified in a distinctive manner. In their sufferings, they made themselves *co-Victims* with Jesus Christ in order to gain graces for many. It could be clearly noticed that they most willingly accept their pains and sufferings for the singular union it has with the passion of Christ. For this reason, they delight in it even though their body aches and groans. In the midst of their pains, the savour the heavenly graces like seeing their Angels, visions and ecstatic experiences that plunge them into supernatural delight. No one eats his cake and still holds it in his hand. We either immerse ourselves into worldly pleasure trying to avoid pain and end up in perpetual darkness of pain or we accept purifying pains that will grant us perpetual bliss in the company of the Holy Angels. THOSE WHO RUN AWAY FROM PAIN OF RIGHTEOUSNESS RUN INTO THE AGONY OF DEMONS, WHILE THOSE WHO ACCEPT TO BE IMMOLATED AS VICTIMS OF RIGHTEOUSNESS MEET WITH ANGELS.

Fourth, all the Saint we presented and other holy people of God have the common attitude of not clinging to the material things of the world. They use the material things without any attachment to it. They lived with a vision that looks beyond the material and the physical. They were all *Wayfarers – Travelers* or *Pilgrims*. Some of them tasted indulgence to world, like Mary of Magdala, St. Augustine, Francis of Assisi, St. Margaret of Cortona, etc. When they encountered the delight of heaven, they lived the rest of their lives in penance and gratitude to God for delivering them. Angels are ministering Spirits sent by God to serve those who are *Wayfarers* and have focused their attention towards their salvation in heaven (Heb. 1:14). Demons are worldly spirits sent to minister to those who focus their attention on the material world. ANGELS ARE MORE REAL TO THOSE HEAVEN-BOUND THAN THOSE ENGROSSED IN MATERIAL WORLD.

Finally, it is not only the things one understands very well that exist for real. There are a lot of things that exist for real but are beyond my comprehension for many reasons.

i)   Either one has not been schooled or trained well to understand them; like the network and movement of the nebulae and galaxies.

ii)   Or, one does not have the instruments that will help me to understand them; like trying to interpret microorganisms in the water with naked eyes (without microscope).

iii)   Or, some reality can never be translated to my human understanding without the help of some equipment; like trying to get the audio or visual frequencies in the airwaves without the help of transistors or satellites. Some one who has no transistor radio can say that there is no radio frequency in his area because he does not hear anything with his naked ear. Likewise, someone who has no satellite dish or antenna could argue that there is no television frequency around his house. It takes installation of either a transistor or a satellite to bring these two contenders to believe that the problem is not in the airwave around them but in what *they have not*.

Therefore, it takes *faith in God* and His Angels, a *burning desire* to make heaven and *love* of these Messengers to experience that they are real. Everyone ought to pray for these graces from

God. THE REALITY OR THE EXISTENCE OF ANGELS DOES NOT DEPEND ON WHETHER ONE BELIEVES IN THEM OR NOT. ANGELS EXIST AND SERVE THOSE WHO IMPLORE THEIR HELP.

CHAPTER THREE

SINNER'S ANGEL – TESTIMONIES OF FAITH

The content of this last chapter is purely subjective. It is not to be taken as a standard for Christian faith in the Angels but a testimony of the little faith of a sinner who believes in the Angels. The desire to study the Angels and try to put down my findings in writing was borne out of my experiences of their ministry in my life. No one is bound to believe my testimony. I proudly share it in sincere appreciation of all the favours I have received from my Angel Guardians. Probably one or two may through this sharing begin to honour and invoke their own Guardian Angels.

Before I share my testimonies, I would like to re-introduce my pastoral commitment that exposed me to these realities. As a seminarian, I was not exposed to the spiritual experiences I encountered after ordination. Most of my contemporaries in the seminary would agree that I am neither spiritual nor prayerful as charismatic ones like Padre Pio who saw his Angels even as a little boy. I was what every body would call *regular*. Thanks to God, I was as normal as every regular person.

With regards to belief in the extraordinary things like Angels and demons, I never doubted or believed more than I was taught in the catechism classes, the seminary formation, and preaching of those I have been opportune to listen. As one who grew up without much crisis to face, I think I neither worried about the threat of demons nor the help of Angels. Besides the regular seminary prayers, which I followed like the rest of the seminarians and the regular family night prayers and morning Masses at home, I did not worry myself about any other prayers. But then, I had a little shift of attention to the spiritual realities around me through the encounters I experienced after my priestly ordination. I will share some of the encounters that made me believe the way I do now in the Angels.

My first awakening to these spiritual realities came just on Monday, 22nd August 1994. I remember this date very well because that was the starting point for me. One of my Aunt's daughters, who was my contemporary and schoolmate, was strangely sick. They have been to hospitals, but she could not be diagnosed of any illness. She ate well and had none of the normal symptoms of fever or typhoid or malaria, etc. She simply moped at people and could not utter a word to anybody. She had been in this situation for weeks before my ordination. Before this sickness began, the last time I met her, she was still normal and she had called me *"fada b'anyi"* (our own family priest), jokingly demonstrating to me the kind of attire she would put on the day of my ordination. So, when her mother visited me to congratulate me a day after my first Mass (Monday, 22nd August 1994, she hugged me happily shouting, *"fada lekwe nwanne gi nwanyi mara ihe i g'eme ya, iburugokwa fada!"* (Now you are priest, see what you could do to help your sister). She begged me to come and see her and see if she would talk to me because she did not to anyone. I promised her I would visit her on my way back from the morning Mass tomorrow because they lived along the way to the Church.

I visited her the next day after Mass as I promised. When I got to the house, I called her as soon as I alighted from the car inside the compound. I continued shouting her name till I got to the room where she was. She sat up when she heard me calling, and was sitting on the bed when I entered the room. She simply looked at me and let out a passing smile without uttering a word. I spent about 30 minutes with her telling her everything I could remember to trigger a word from her, but all she would do at best was to make her face and change her position of sitting. I was sure she heard me well from her non-verbal reactions but she could not utter a word. I got up and walked into the corridor disappointed. I stood for few minutes in the corridor thinking of what to do. I did not see her as sick enough to be anointed. Actually, she looked very healthy and they said she ate well. And if she woulld not be anointed with oil of the sick, what should a priest do for a person like this? Here was the beginning of my problem. I started to feel just at the first call of my ministry as a priest that I was incapacitated or was failing. The mother was waiting for me outside beside my car to know what I would like to do. She had told me the day before that she believed that her case was (*ogbanje*) diabolical, not medical. I could not think of anything then. I simply told her as I entered my car to leave that till I come back tomorrow. I left with confusion and worry in my heart. She just spoilt my ordination euphoria.

Remember different people react to the same stimulus in different ways depending on their perception and judgment of the stimulus. At that point of my experience, I judged the situation more as a failure on my part; either, I did not learn enough in the seminary on how to minister to people like her, or I did not have enough faith in me to discern if her case was actually diabolical or medical. I had no one available to consult. The Parish Priest has already left for holidays, leaving the Masses for the newly ordained. There were no mobile or land phones then to call him. I was stuck. I could not eat well that Monday, nor joyfully attend to visitors still coming to congratulate me. Every little space I had alone, my mind got back to that room. In the evening after supper, the next day was fast approaching and still I did not know what to do. I decided to get to the field behind our compound with my rosary to pray for her. I said the rosary several times without counting the mysteries any more. I earnestly begged Our Lady to let me understand something at the beginning of my priestly duties. I would like to know if what the mother was saying is true. I asked Mary mother of God to give me, at least, a sign to organize myself for this ministry. If wicked forces disturb her, I begged Mother Mary; she should talk to me as soon as I enter that room tomorrow because light should automatically dispel darkness. But if she did not talk to me, I will take it that she had medical issues, and I was going to take her to the hospital myself. She should spare me confusion at least. That night, I realized that crisis and difficult circumstances could make one pray for a long time with concentrated attention.

No need to tell you how I slept that night. The morning was very long in coming. I remembered I was up hours before the Mass. I got to the Church very early, did my morning office and the Mass. I arrived at her house, jumped out without locking my car and hurried to her room shouting her name. To the glory of God and to my spiritual elation, she responded and talked with me normally. I did not recite any prayer there. The mother was as surprised as I was. I did not tell the mother anything. She was there and she saw everything. She even forgot to ask me what next as she conversed with her daughter. I left with more joy than I ever had since my two days of ordination. From this incident, my commitment to priestly life changed. Now, that I am sharing this story, all those who knew me during the seminary days and who always asked me jokingly "Is Saul among the Prophets too?" you know where I am coming from now. That experience made me to believe in my rosary, believe in Mother Mary, and my priesthood more than any teacher, preacher, or school ever did. The rest of the story I am about to share in this study started from this encounter. It is a story of one who was lukewarm, a young inexperienced priest whom it pleased God through the motherly intercession of Mary to grant few experiences to help his lukewarm faith to improve. I know I am vulnerable with this sharing. I am not afraid of being misunderstood or misinterpreted. The purpose is simply to encourage people to believe not in the power of demons but in the presence and assistance of the Holy Angels.

3.1 CHALLENGED TO STAY AWAKE IN PRAYERS

After one month of relief duty, I arrived at St. Peter's Adazi Ani to begin my first priestly assignment as a vicar under Late Monsignor Philip Chinyere (May God rest his soul!). All who knew Monsignor Chinyere knew how thorough and organized he was as a pastor. Of course, he gave me my duties properly written out. I was not in doubt of what to do and how to carry it out because Monsignor, also the Diocesan Judicial Vicar then, properly believe in legally spelling of duties to his vicars. That was another fortunate thing that God granted me, starting the work with one who helped me to be properly footed in pastoral duties of a priest. We actually had a wonderful pastoral collaboration so much so that Monsignor loosened some of his *don'ts* with me.

Everything went on normal until the week Monsignor had to travel to one of the northern States for their annual Canon Law Society's week. I was left alone with the junior seminarian on apostolic work, two houseboys, and the cook to manage the Parish. You know how it feels to be the master of the house for one week. The evening of the same day Monsignor left, I came down as usual to the refectory to have my supper. I was dishing out the food, when the lady who served as our cook, came in to tell me something she felt could not wait till I finish my meal. I learnt from Monsignor that she has been hired for barely a year. When she said there was something she wanted to tell me, of course, I told her to wait till I have finished my meal without looking up at her. But I was wrong. That food was not eaten. I cannot say how it began, but I was startled up to see the lady spinning around and crashing unto the cupboard, to the refrigerator, to the sink and landed on the floor scattering things along. At first, I panicked! What kind of trick is this? I was now standing and shouting, "What is that?" The lady seemed to be in another world battling with something invisible to my eyes. As she started rolling again on the floor with her dress all turned, exposing her inner wears, I ran out to call the seminarian to be another witness to this. The seminarian came with me surprised and confused what happened between us. I had no time to explain that I knew nothing because she began talking to some people we could not see, punching her fists in the air and putting up what looked to us like she was fighting back and calling strange names. To cut the long story short, I convinced the seminarian to help me to pull her up to the sitting room for better space.

The seminarian, now one of the priests of the diocese, stood by me till about 3 am as we experienced the strangest night ever. The encounter is better experienced than described. If I was not there seeing with my own eyes, I will not believe anybody narrating the story to me. The summary is that I was led to encounter a person under the attack of the evil spirits. Describing what happened here is not relevant to our study. Just that I experienced firsthand encounter with forces of darkness at work in a person. You can imagine how the next few days would go in the absence of the pastor. We (I and the seminarian) did not sleep next few days as things were unfolding and we have been involved and could not back off.

By the time the pastor came back, through the grace of God, things were gotten under control because we were challenged to stay awake praying for her all nights during the week. I narrated the encounter to the pastor, he threatened to send her away, but I begged him to leave it to me since she wanted to be helped. Monsignor allowed her because I begged, but promised to keep extra eye on her from then. I told this story because, from that day, I was challenged to stay awake praying because of the things I saw and heard.

Several weeks had passed and I was beginning to digest that encounter with the cook when one Sunday afternoon, after the 9.30 a.m. Mass, I was called down to the sitting room by the Monsignor. There were with him a lady and a young girl of about 18 years whom she said was their house help. When I sat down, Monsignor signaled to the lady to repeat her story. She told me that another woman, who was her next neighbour, reported her house help to have fought and beaten the neighbour's little boy as they were returning from the children's (8.00 am) Mass. This woman told me, "Fr, can you imagine that! Nkechi (the house help) was sleeping right inside the room and never left the compound before my neighbour came screaming". Nkechi's landlady told me she was cooking outside and Nkechi never left the compound for the children's Mass. Both attended the early Mass together and came back together (6. 00 a.m.). The woman said that what surprised her most was that as the neighbour turned in anger threatening to go back to the scene of the fight and deal with Nkechi herself, she went into the room and found Nkechi asleep on her bed. She ran back pleading with the neighbour to come back. The neighbour returned and saw the same Nkechi she left at the scene of the fight in the room. The neighbour was frightened according to Nkechi's landlady. She left with her son, calling her *Ogbanje* (a re-incarnate) and *Amosu* (a witch). She then added, "Fr. I came down to report to you people this time because this one is beyond me". She recalled that several times, other children have told her that Nkechi, sometimes, frightened them with snakes but she has never taken it seriously. She wanted us to do something because she cannot understand how she can bi-locate and fight. When she finished her story, Monsignor looked up at me and said, "Fr, over to you, I am going to rest against the evening program". He left me with the landlady and Nkechi. Just put yourself in my shoes. A young priest who was not taught any of these stuffs in the seminary, facing all these within the space of four months after ordination.

I promised God after my niece's case at home that I will always live up to every challenge I meet along the way since they made me to understand that these spiritual issues are real. So when I remembered that I should not back off, I took Nkechi with her landlady into the rectory chapel, although I was not sure what I was going to do. Getting inside the chapel, I knelt down to say some prayers with them. The landlady knelt too, but Nkechi refuse to kneel down. Instead, she put her two hands in her waist as if to say, what can you do? When I turned and saw the snobbish posture, I ordered her sternly to kneel down. She still refused. The landlady raised her voice in command, but she was unmoved. I became angry. I always had a cane at the back of my car which was for pursuing catechism kids, or when I visit block rosary centers or see some pupils idling late to school in the mornings. I went to my car, which was parked close to the chapel, pulled out the cane, and threatened to strike if she refused to kneel. (Do not judge these actions, they were according to the zeal of the young priest inexperienced in these matters). She still adamantly looked at me from head to toe inviting me with her eyes to do my worst. You can feel the rage in me at that point. I gave her a mild stroke at first. She burst into laughing without any sign of pain. I then walloped her thoroughly with the cane all over but she clapped her hand and danced mockingly at me without any feeling of pain. I stopped and turned to the tabernacle with inner feeling of "Lord, this insult is too much to take from whoever this girl is in your presence". Whether this was a good prayer or not at that point, that was all I could do. By the way, flogging a person in the chapel would look weird to the Western world but it is not out of place in training a child in our culture.

Instantly, I had a flash of thought pushing me to go back to my car, pull my sick call bag out, rub off a little of the oil for catechumens (I thought at that moment was oil for exorcism) in my hands, smeared it on the cane and came back striking her this time with my enraged spirit. She then got it, shouted in pain, knelt down begging me to stop. Well, while theologians and liturgist can debate on my action, all I knew then was that when David took and ate the bread for priests, he needed it to stay alive (cf. 1 Sam. 26:6). I was happy turning over the control of things to my side. I prayed a bit. And dismissed then, promising the landlady as they were leaving that I will continue to pray for her. Nkechi left the chapel shouting, "pray for yourself, not me, because I will teach you a lesson in this town". It was this threat that actually made me to narrate this story. From that moment, I knew I had no option than to cut my sleep, stay awake and pray for these two girls (our cook and Nkechi).

Could you believe that three days, on Wednesday after that Sunday, I was in the same chapel alone in the evening praying for them; all of a sudden, Nkechi walked into the chapel and started renting at me to stop praying for her. The rest of the encounter with her remains a big lesson that opened me up to believe in supernatural powers. To the glory of God, she gave in, was baptized, and delivered. I started with my negative encounters to let the reader know how I got to experience the work of the Angels. My remaining stories will show how the heavenly Spirits intervened to assist me as I struggled with the pastoral encounters coming my way.

3.2 MY GRIGIO BARKS.

Remember I narrated above how our cook got me into praying for her deliverance from mermaid spirits that was attacking her? My first experience with dogs acting out in the face of unseen forces was one night in those fateful days when we were praying for the cook's deliverance. The Pastor, Monsignor Chinyere, has returned and was at home. The junior seminarian, now a priest, and the other two houseboys, were all sleeping. Monsignor had two dogs that were released every night to keep watch. That particular night, the dogs barked so uncontrollably for a long time that everybody got out of bed disturbed; what could have caused such unusual barking? Surprisingly, there was nothing or anybody the dogs were barking at. Yet, even when we were out, the dogs could hardly be restrained. None of us understood this.

Monsignor was in particular worried and he jokingly said to me, "Are you sure it is not your friends attacking the cook?" He meant, the mermaids attacking our cook. He was right because the next morning the cook confessed that they would have killed her that night had not the dogs waken us up to scare them away. She said that they left her when Monsignor shouted the name of the seminarian from his room window upstairs asking why the dogs were barking. This experience did not make much sense to me until I read the book, *All about the Angels*, written by Fr. Paul O'Sullivan. In the book, I read the story of Don Bosco and his *il Grigio*. Remember I told the story of Don Bosco's friend and protector, *il Grigio*?

My own experience was not like Don Bosco's, but I saw the protecting hand of some Holy Beings at work. It happened that I was posted to be the Pastor of Christ the King Parish Adazi Nnukwu in October 1999. I got to the parish and took up the apostolate. I was to begin the parish because it was newly created. Everything was new. The rectory was still under construction. I stayed in a temporary residence while administering the parish. I was fond of dogs. So I bought a good Alsatian puppy of six weeks from a Vet Doctor at a scandalously high price. The dog was lovely and healthy. After three months, I sent it to the police college Enugu for training because I wanted it mannered. But, I lost the dog after a month with the police. They simply could not tell what happened to it. But I could see how devastated the police in charge was because of the dog. He confessed that he has been handling dogs for many years now and could not understand how a healthy dog could take ill overnight and die. It pained me so much, but I accepted it without suspecting anything spiritual.

It was after the Christmas crusade-prayers and a series of encounters we had earlier in the parish that culminated in a serious threat to my life (my ordination car got burnt during this period). In the heat of these spiritual encounters, one of my adversaries who claimed she was powerful and will deal with me with her water spirits told me precisely without any connection in the dispute at hand that she was responsible for killing my dog. I asked where the dog was when they killed it; she told me how that night the police passed the usual ration of food to the dog and they poisoned it spiritually. The dog ate it and died. This looks fairy, but what I passed through that period especially the encounter we had during the crusade made me not to dismiss the possibility. How could anybody explain the engine block of the generator we were using for the crusade to brake up in pieces like a glass tumbler? Usually, mechanical malfunctioning of the engine block will cause the block to grind and stop working, not to burst into pieces. My parishioners who were close, especially those who worked with me, could be witnesses of what I am writing. My stories are verifiable because many of the actors are still alive. So because of these encounters, I took the lady's boast of killing my dog seriously.

I got another dog after some months from Jos. This time, I am not to take chances. Immediately I got home, based on what I read from Fr. O'Sullivan's Angels' story, I took my six weeks old puppy into my chapel, and prayed over it consecrating it to my Guardian Angel and to Our Lady. I asked Our Lady to protect it from any spiritual or physical threat to its life and asked my Guardian Angel to possess it and use it spiritually and physically to ward of unseen enemies around the rectory. When I was asked the name of the dog, I said *Grigio*. My parishioners did not know this inside story, but they admired and feared *Grigio* so much. I sent it for few months training at a private handler at Onitsha and it came back healthy, huge and strong.

One day someone came to me and without knowing anything about my dead and present dogs, asked from where I got my dog. I was surprised at the question because it had no relevance to what she came for. When I insisted she had to tell me why the question, she confessed that she wanted to know how the dog got its extraordinary powers. I became more curious and wanted her to explain. She then told me that I may not believe it; several groups of my spiritual enemies have complained of the dog not allowing them around the Church compound anymore. She told me that one night, she was in the company of forces sent to come and attack me at night. But they were still a good distance from the rectory compound when *Grigio* started barking with flames of fires issuing from its mouth unto them. They took to their heels and for her that confirmed the earlier experiences of others who attempted it. This story look fairy enough, but from that moment, I knew how much I am protected for believing in the story of Don Bosco's *Grigio*. I did not narrate these kinds of stories to people or in the congregations because it would cause much debate and row. But now I am giving it as my Angel testimony. These Good Spirits have been so kind to me that I need to let the world know about them even if they ridicule my story. My Guardian Angels used my dog to protect me on several occasions. Knowing that Angels are around me in such stories, like this visitor who told me about my dog, strengthened my belief in them. Sometimes it seems like you are imagining them, but when they act and you see the result, you cannot doubt their presence.

3.3 FLOGGED TO IDENTIFY HERSELF

This story happened in January 2000 after the Christmas activities. The new parish I was in charge had a special Christmas prayers organized for those returning from abroad. We ended the prayers and other Christmas events almost spent in energy. The next preoccupation for me was the forthcoming novena to my patron Saint's feast on January 20. Usually, I make it a day to share what I have generously with my parishioners by celebrating Mass and entertaining them with foods.

The novena started on January 11 and was some days into it when I had a visitor. One of my seminarians (I was posted from Spiritual Year Formation house to the parish) from a family very close to me came with her niece to the parish. He had wanted to bring her to me before Christmas but I told him that was a busy period for me. The seminarian reported to me that the family believes that something is wrong with the girl since she behaves in strange manners. He told me that the father would kill the girl because of her behaviour if he (the seminarian) left her behind with the father. In fact, he showed me the scare in the girl's hand where the father poured hot water on her. In summary, she was brought for rehabilitation or whatever we can do to tame her behaviour. I told the seminarian to leave her with us and go back to the seminary. He did. Without suspecting anything, I asked the girl to squat with the others in the quarters and join in the novena we were doing. That will tell you how blind I was to supernatural realities. I intended to give her attention when I find the space. I also wanted her to pray with us for few days before I could talk with her. Remember, I had no ministry going on. Mine was simply, normal parish setting. The only thing peculiar was that I involved everyone around me, including the cook in our regular daily prayers. You are bound as long as you are with us – the cook, my housekeeper, and visitors who hung around for one need or the other. I never expelled anybody provided you join in what was going on.

After the second or third day the girl arrived, I had not yet found time to talk with her. A lot of things were still taking my attention. It should be the sixth or seventh day into the novena. I was in my private chapel upstairs with my little family in praise-worship to the Lord in the Blessed Sacrament in preparation before moving to the Church for the novena. All of a sudden, the girl (brought by the seminarian) ran up into the chapel interrupting our prayers with her screaming; "*have mercy on me, please! Please! Please! I beg you! I have withdrawn my statement! Fr! Fr! Please stop him, I won't do it again!*" Believe me, we were about five people in the chapel praying.   We all stopped, confused, and looking at her surprised. Nobody understood her or saw who was flogging her. She finally fell to the floor of the chapel panting and crying. I asked the people with me to start going to the Church to get things ready for the novena and I will join them shortly. When they left, I pulled up the girl who looked completely deflated like a balloon released of air from the valve. She could hardly sit down or open her eyes. As I knew I had little time now, I prayed within me to Jesus in the Eucharist to use this opportunity to let her reveal what was wrong in her life with her own mouth. She started talking to me.

> I am sorry Fr I was wrong. I thought you were so simple and easy to get. They sent me here to kill you. I was prepared specially to succeed this time after the first group failed during the Christmas crusade-prayers. They told me you are difficult and terrible. I thought you would recognize who I was or see what was put in me against you when I came. On the contrary, you saw nothing and you looked normal and simple. So this evening, when my members saw I was alone in the room they came to me (she meant in spiritual form) and we were discussing, I boasted to them to relax, before I could finish saying...the man is not as you painted him, I will finish him before he knows it... a flash of light appeared in the room and all my members fled. Then that terrible man in white started whipping me for making that statement about you. He is terrible and merciless. Please Fr beg him not to flog me again...

Honestly, it's been a long time, I may not have quoted all verbatim because I was not copying them down, but that was almost what I heard from the girl. You can imagine the feeling of joy in me as I was going for the novena that evening. I took her from the chapel to the Church for the novena and we spent more time in the Church praying to my Patron Saint and honouring the Angels, especially, my ever watchful and protective Angels. The rest of the girl's stay was for me another lesson for life. Many people who witnessed the rest of the girl's story of deliverance are still alive today in Adazi Nnukwu and could bear testimony to this. She got a nickname while staying in my house.

Who do you think flogged her? Was the girl faking? Of course, what followed her confession proved that she was not. I may not be able to tell the whole story here. I simply want to testify to how my Guardian Angels intervened even when I was not conscious of what was going on around me. Do not forget, when the Angels of light are not around, demons of darkness could be threatening! But when the heavenly Guards are at post, darkness and its forces are under us. It is better to seek the favour of the Angels than to live in fear of trying to escape from human or spiritual demons.

3.4 FLOGGED TO PRAY

Yet this is another fairy-like story. Two years after the above incident (end of the year 2002), I met a couple that had long marital problems. By God's special assistance, it was exposed that the wife was involved as a member of the spiritually wicked sects. Initially the family members thought it was the man who had problems with his life style. When I took the wife to prayers before the Blessed Sacrament, she confessed and admitted before her mother and husband that she was responsible for the accident that took her father's life. To cut the long story short, after many days of deliverance prayers, I started to rehabilitate her by teaching her how to pray and instructing her on the values of the Gospel so that she could withstand the attempt to pull her back to the sect. She stayed for some time with her kids and husband with us going through sessions of prayers. When I felt it was time for her to go back home (Onitsha), I called her and warned her seriously that if she does not continue the prayers consistently every day as she had been doing while staying with us, she would definitely be drawn back. She promised she would continue the prayers. I ask her, "Would you like my Guardian Angel to flog you into prayers any night you omit praying out of your own laziness?" She accepted the deal. I told her it was not a joke, that she would be embarrassed if she failed and we had the deal. They went home.

Barely two weeks after, she came back humbled. She narrated her story: She started feeling that everything she went through while she was with us happened very fast, leaving her with little options. Now at home, she was beginning to feel that she might not continue in this "church-thing", as she tagged it. So she started to omit the prayers. The first night was okay but the second night as she told me, "I am not sure if it was a dream or not, but you were there in your white cassock and a long cane, and you started beating me asking why I stopped praying. I only realized myself when my mother told me to stop shouting the reverend father's name and disturbing their neighbours because she could not see anybody flogging me." She said she was calling my name begging me to stop flogging her, promising that she will start praying again. She ended by asking me how did I know that she stopped praying and how did I get there to flog her. I was speechless and felt highly unworthy of the story. I simply told her that it was not I, but my Angel using my face to keep our deal real. The mother confirmed the encounter; she said she heard her shouting my name when she got to her room; she was running around the room trying to avoid invisible beating and begging me to stop. "I thought she was going mental" was what she made out of the whole scene. The lady is still alive and would have been accessed for confirmation if not for anonymity. *Ihe onye kporo nkita ya k'onaza* – Your dog respond to whatever name you give it. My Angels are true and real in spite of me. It is something wonderful to think about. It humbles one to imagine such a divine favour and gift.

3.5 WARNED NEVER TO MAKE ANY ATTEMPT

I left for studies from my parish after the fifth year (2004). It was years of continuous encounter with God and the people of God in many respects. I got opportunity to further my studies and I left for studies in Rome. I am telling this story because even abroad, my watchful Holy Guardians did not abandon me. The change of environment, the language, the people and the study took a lot of toll on me. I would want to emphasize that it was not what I expected. I thought life would be a lot easy over there, but it was not though in different perspective – the issues were more of academics, language, food and culture shock.

By the special grace of God, I did not quit. I was almost a year into my doctoral research when I received a call from somebody I know residing in America telling me that she gave my number to somebody who needed spiritual help. She said that this person was her schoolmate. This mate complained to her about some spiritual issues she felt I could be of help. The lady later called me and we discussed her issues. From the discussion, I thought the lady was giving up on God and in the power of God to intervene in her life. I tried to transfer through scriptural passages some hope into her. I knew I was strongly affirmative and positive in the conversation trying to stir up her depressing spirit. Whatever transpired in the spiritual during our conversation, I was innocent of that because I knew nothing more. I was surprised when the friend who introduced her to me called me back asking what I told the lady because, according to her, this lady was eager to know "what makes me as bold and as sure as I was of the things I said to her". I was taken aback at this. Was she seeking for help or was she sizing me? Anyway, the next encounters I had with the lady through phone were more of "bring what you have on!" None of us said it openly, but we felt it in the conversation. I got the feeling that she believed nothing here on earth could help her out, but I was sure her case was under God's control and I did not mince words in telling her this either from the scriptures or from my little experience of what God could do and is still doing. To cut the long story short, the lady decided that she was flying to Rome to see things for herself. I mean I do not want to narrate the whole details of her personal issues.

She came to Rome. I went to the airport and met her, took her to the convent near our college, where she lodged. I first realized whom I was dealing with when she said to me after we collected the key from the receptionist and was going to the lifter, "why are all these dead people around here?" I was seeing nothing. I asked her, "Where are they?" She looked as if to say to me, "are you so blind that you cannot see them?" Well, from my past experience, you do not want to get into argument with somebody not functioning within your own space. So, I immediately said, "okay, even if they are here, we have authority over them". So I prayed commanding whatever she was seeing to disappear, and she relaxed and said they have gone. Remember, I am not here to prove whether she saw anything or not but just to say something was seriously wrong somewhere with her.

We spent some days visiting and praying in holy places outside Rome. We went to St. Francis of Assisi, St. Rita of Cassia and other tourist centres in Rome. She left after ten intensive days of walking which was the greatest penance she had as one coming from where you drive to every place. I thought I did my best playing the host and the interpreter because she could not do anything without my presence because of the language. Of course, I knew something was happening in her life as we went through these normal prayers, pilgrimages and tours. I never doubted the mysterious ways God works although I can never explain or know them. You can imagine how relieved I was as I was escorting her back to the airport.

When she got back. She called and affirmed that I was right in all I ever told her. She then told me something more – the main reason for narrating this story. She said that before she left for Rome, she had a visitation. A *Celestial Being* with imposing aura confronted her and warned her that her visit to Rome will be beneficial to her if she did not make any attempt to harm the priest. She said that the visitor promised her that any attempt would spell her doom. As she said to me, "I have lived through troubles and strange beings, and I know a good threat when I meet one. This visitor was something else. You are truly favoured and protected", she summarized.

I did not need her to tell me how favoured I am with regard to the unworthy blessings I have received from God. But I was happy to hear it again especially from a foreigner. Whatever was at work in her was definitely strong. I do not want to get into that here. There is something very strange in a person who can tell the exact character of someone she never met in her life. When she was in Rome, this lady described to me the characters of all my priest friends who greeted her and people acquainted to me that we met. She never saw them before. That actually made me believe she was probably seeing something for real. Otherwise, how could she be that accurate with different persons? Let her personal issues be by the way.

The point remains, who was that visitor and why would she be warned even when I knew nothing about it. You can doubt your own Angel, I BELIEVE IN MINE. THEY ARE REAL AND SO GOOD TO A SINNER LIKE ME TOO.

CHAPTER FOUR

QUEEN OF THE ANGELS

4.1   INTRODUCTION

By the time I finish this story, you will be convinced that I am out of my senses. But am not alone in this madness (cf Mk. 3:21). I would not mind being mad for this Woman whose love and protection is still keeping me alive today. What man out there is not madly in love with the woman of his life? I will take any ridicule for MY LADY. I am convinced that many will be attracted to her sharing my story.

When I started work as the pastor of Christ the King Parish, Adazi Nnukwu in 1999, I undertook some prayer commitments with youthful zeal. I even called out young ebullient boys and girls (nicknamed – *Obuaja* group) who were willing to join me in continuous intercessory prayers for the parish and for those who needed our prayers. With this group, we initiated continuous night prayers on daily basis (except Saturdays and Sundays) that was lasting from 11.00 p.m till 4.00am. Such was our zeal. The intercessions stirred up many things in the parish and in the town. One of which was the story I am now telling. A humbling encounter, I believe, permitted by Our Lady, Mary mother of God to teach me something I would have hardly learnt fast in normal circumstances.

Before I begin the story, let me remark that my father made me to be saying my rosary every day by force as a little boy. He dragged me to the morning mass everyday, come rain or shine and I must recite the rosary with him along the road as we went. So when I was entering the junior seminary, he warned me sternly to always say it everyday. I would not want to lie to him whenever I came back on holidays that I was still saying it. So every night that we did not say the rosary in common in the seminary, I will just pick up my rosary and thumb through the fifty beads, saying only "Hail Mary" on each bead without completing the rest of the prayer. This habit helped to assure my conscience that I was saying the rosary. However, it helped me to be attached to the rosary more than any other prayers we had in the manuals for seminarian. Few months before coming to the parish, I did total consecration to Mary according to St. Louis de

Monfort to become a "slave of Mary"[185]. I am giving these backgrounds so that you will understand well the encounter I had in my story. I am not that pious; I was convinced and led into this consecration by a Seminarian (now a priest) I respected so much for who he was. I had always been led or persuaded into the spiritual devotions I found myself. It is only now that I am beginning to appreciate these people and what they did in my life.

4.2   AN ENCOUNTER WITH THE 'PROFESSIONAL'

The parish was just a little above seven months old. But within this time, I have had numerous encounters both public and private. One of the private encounters began one evening when my little family (those staying in the rectory) came together for our evening prayers. Usually we recite the Rosary, some Psalms and worship songs together. Sometimes, depending on the occasion and need, we add some words of encouragement. So this fateful evening, I remarked to my family that I noticed that the harmony in the household was not as it used to be. For restoration of peace and harmony, I encourage all present in the Chapel to publicly ask for forgiveness of anybody he has hurt and to forgive all who have hurt him. I started with myself and turned to the next person at my right because we were sitting in a circle with hand interlocked. It continued till it reached the turn of one of my nephews who visited and was lodging with us that period. He did not talk. We waited for him for few minutes and he kept his head down and eyes closed speechless. I signaled to the next person to continue ignoring him because I did not want his problem to distract the reconciliation. When he noticed that he was ignored, he untied his hands from the circle and left the Chapel. When we finished the round (eight people in all), I encouraged all to go for personal confession within the week and we concluded the prayers.

I was going down to the refectory for my supper when I remembered my nephew who left the Chapel. I decided to look for him to find out what was the matter. I least suspected anything serious. I found him lying on the bed in their room facing the wall. I stood at the edge

<hr>

[185] Not many people like the word 'slave'. But this is "holy slavery of love". Search out the teaching of St. Louis the Monfort on this – it simply means one who has given himself and all about him to Mary to live solely under Her control. To do everything *with* Her, *through* Her, *in* Her and *for* Her. It means, with my whole heart Oh Mother, I submit myself to belong to you and be led by you to love your Son Jesus Christ in more fitting way.

of the bed and called his name. He remained still. I repeated his name this time louder. No reaction still. I stooped over and shook him strongly, he turned gradually like a robot with fixed limbs and said, "don't disturb me", in a hoarse masculine voice like that of forty-five year old man. My nephew should be fifteen or sixteen year old that time. Immediately, I realized that I have company in the house I have met series of this lately. I called his name again reminding him that it was I, Father that was calling him. He sat on the bed reclining to the wall and folding his legs into position of one about to do *yoga* meditation. He opened his eyes and it was glittering like one who has taken half bottle of rum at a time. He smiled sinisterly at me and said in the same hoarse but calm voice, *"I know it is you. What do you want?"* I held myself from anger because I am suspecting something foul here. I replied, *"What is wrong with you?"*

"Wrong with me or you?" the voice counter-questioned me.

"By the way, who are you?" my spirit picked up to challenge the voice.

"If you want to know who I am, sit down and let us talk, I am not to be commanded by dust like you," the voice retorted.

That statement confirmed to me that it was not my nephew talking. Of course, he would never address me that way. So I raise my voice in prayer demanding his identity,

"I command you in the name of Jesus Christ of Nazareth, who are you?" He busted out laughing. He said in laughter, *"look at you, mere dust, commanding a spirit like me. Do you realize you are dus*t?" He scornfully demanded. I ignored his ridicule and started praying the way I knew, thinking within me that only prayer will overcome whomever this insolent demon might be. While I was still praying, the voice came again as an advise to me,

"Dust, you better sit down and let us talk, listen, I am the Professional, I am not like the others you had been handling. I have monitored this house for seven months now. I got my chance this morning in the sacristy...(he told me what my nephew did in the sacristy that morning)...*If you do not sit down and we talk, I will kill this boy by midnight and by the time you send the body back to your sister at Achina, you will decide whether to continue deliverance or not…"*

As his voice was rising with pride and arrogance in the speech, I remembered I should not allow the devil to dictate the tone of the interaction. So I stepped up now in a higher tone,

"You are a liar, you have always been arrogant and boastful… I invoke in the mighty name of Jesus Holy Ghost Fire…"

"Not with me, dust! I told you that I am different. I have never been in the flesh. I came from the fire…I am the Professional…" he continued his boasts.

At this point, I felt I needed some sacramental to help the fight. So, I stepped out of the door of the room, called out for holy water. When he saw the container in my hand, he said,

"I told you I am different, bring the water here into the mouth, I will drink it". I poured out some holy water into the mouth and he swallowed and remained calm. I was shocked because, I have gotten used to seeing violent reactions of demons in deliverance sections when holy water or Holy Ghost Fire is used. This situation became troublesome to me. I decided within me without saying a word that I am going up to the Chapel to bring down the Blessed Sacrament, let me see how he would not react to it. I could scarcely turn to leave the room when I heard his warning,

"Dust, if you bring that thing here, I'll take it from you and crush it!"

Well, I have never been through such a hard demon…motionless at the invocation of Holy Ghost Fire and drinking holy water. I had no courage in me anymore to bring the Blessed Sacrament. I didn't want it desecrated. My spirit was down and almost helpless. The voice started rattling again, seeing that I was troubled,

"Listen to me dust, I heard you invoking Michael and their stuff…I said I am the Professional, do you know I was ranked with him, I can always fight him…"

I could not take all his boasts anymore, I became angry with myself and my God for allowing this demon to sit here and rattle insults at my belief and me. Instantly, in what looked like a flash of intuition, a voice within me asked 'have you forgotten that you are a slave of Mary, have you invoked Her?' The reaction to this inner voice was both ways; just as I started kneeling down to apologize to Mary mother of Jesus for not going through her as all her slaves ought to do, for the first time since the encounter began, the demon showed violent reaction. He must have read my mind because as I started a hymn to honour Mary, he threw himself (in my nephew's body of course) out of the bed and stood in the space in a frontal way screaming,

"*That Woman again! Call Her! I will fight Her! She is a wicked Woman but I will fight her…*"

You could sense immediately the frustration and despair in the voice now. Of course my spirit was inflamed and I ignored him completely now vibrating in my favorite praise of Her,

"*Ave Maria, Maria Nne mooooooh, Maria, Maria Nne m…*"

I have started clapping my hands and my voice grew higher and stronger, one of the parishioners who joined in the evening prayer and who brought the holy water to me, hearing my singing at this point stepped into the room and joined in the hymn clapping also. Then the drama started. We saw my nephew flipped from one end of the room to the other crashing things as he went. The voice continued talking to 'THE WOMAN' only he was seeing:

"*You are a wicked Woman, how can you tell me, your fellow spirit to obey dust? No, he is dust. I wont obey him. You are very wicked…*"

This continued for about few minutes. I was so afraid that the boy would be seriously wounded from the banging at the wall. He was throwing his fists into the air in a frantic effort to defend himself. We continued the praises to Mary. Finally, I heard the voice saying,

"*Okay, dust give your command, I will obey… you are a wicked Woman…*"

As soon as I heard that, I stopped clapping and singing, and commanded the demon to sit down at the empty corner of the room. He did grumbling still at the "Woman" we were not seeing with him. I knelt down and briefly in prayer recommitted my slavery to Mary pleading that she takes complete control as I question the demon. I begged her on my part, to control my mind so that I will ask the relevant questions and on the part of the demon to hold him so that he is forced to answer correctly the questions without thwarting the truth. I said this prayer because the demon during his boasting raised a lot of issues around me that I wanted clarified now that Our Lady has granted me the control.

Believe this or not, I spent the next hour and a quarter asking the demon questions and he answered all with painful regrets. It was in this encounter that I was schooled on how Angels are classified (though in non theological way) and similarly how demons are graded and grouped. He gave me example of Guardian Angels with the people in my house, implying that a person's spiritual inclination and behaviour depend strongly on the rank of Angel(s) or demon(s) surrounding the person. The discussion ranged through the spiritual activities that have been going on in the parish and around the rectory for the last seven months. He made me to understand the spiritual nature of the town and what we needed to do (of course, the devil offering solution against himself indicated that he was under control). Before, I asked the Queen Mother to take him to his proper place for destruction, I said to the demon in ridicule,

"Why were you, the almighty Professional, jerking at the mention of the Name of Mary?"

He grimed in deep groan and retorted,

"She is a wicked Woman, very wicked, She has all in Her, She can deal with anyone easily. Do not rejoice too much dust, you are not like Her. Pay attention very well to virtues not power if you want to continue in fighting forces. They will catch you one day; very soon, any day She turns her back on you. Remember always that more spiritual activities are going on around you than the physical activities. I promise they will get you one day…"

I thanked my Precious Mother so much for Her intervention and assistance and begged Her to make sure that the-so-called-Professional and his intrigues in the boy was completely removed without any side effect in his body, psyche, mind and spirit. Before, I could finish the prayer, my nephew got himself and was surprised at the condition of the room and our hymn of thanksgiving to Mary.

While you are digesting this encounter, I will now combine the information I got from the encounter and my study of the Angels to tell you something serious about the singular gift God gave the world that changed human condition from the condemned to the redeemed; from slavery to free children of God; from shame to glory; from poverty of grace to heavenly riches; from the wounded to the healed; from nobody (dust) to royalty (Prince and Princes) and from death to life in the spirit. That gift is the ***Immaculate Vessel*** through which Jesus came to us, ***Mary Mother of God***. Now She lives as the ***Queen of Angels*** and of the Church, the body of Jesus Christ Her son. I am a member of that body and, probably, you are too. Let us talk about her in relation to the Angels.

4.3   MARY QUEEN OF THE ANGELS...

There is a Woman I love so much…

There is a Woman I love…

There is a Woman I love so much…

Her Name is Mary…

M-a-r-y, Mamma mhh…, M-a-r-y, Virgin M-a-r-y, Mamma I love.

In the first part of this study (cf. sub title 2.2.3), I mentioned that God shares His communicable attributes with Angels and men. The Angels have higher attributes of the gift of God than men because they are spirits that do not have flesh (dust) like us. That is why when an Angel loves God, the love is pure and constant unlike men whose love changes from day to day depending on the extent the human appetites and will submit to the spirit of God in man. While Angels have higher attributes of divine gifts than men, Mary has higher attribute of divine gift than any Angel. The reason is because while Angels possess divine gifts in parts that complement each other according to divine ordering, Mary possesses in Her the fullness of these gifts. That is the meaning of the statement in the above story by the '*Professional*', "*She has all in Her…*"

No Angel has body, but Mary had body. Her body was of equal purity with Angelic *being* because She has no stain of sin in Her. She shares with the Angels their purity but possessed a flesh (the original dust from which Adam was fashioned) exempt from divine curse (Gen 3:15) making Her more tangible than any Angel. Not only that She possessed the flesh, which no Angel has, the attributes, which the Angels possess in part, Mary possesses in full. For example, the Seraphim possess the highest love of God than other Angels and radiate this love to others. The Cherubim possess the deep knowledge of the mystery of God than others and radiate this grace to others. The Thrones possess the splendour of divine glory and radiates this to others and so on. None of these ranks possess the attributes of others together in themselves in full. Only Mary is favoured to have all together in Her. That was why in his greeting Archangel Gabriel reminded Mary how blessed She was; "Hail *highly*/*most favoured* One, the **Lord is with you**…" (Lk 1:28). The 'favour' God granted Mary is full and highest; no other human being here on earth and nor Angel in heaven received it. The Lord was with Mary not in the sense of standing by her to help and assist Her like other creatures, the Lord was with Her in the real sense of taking flesh from Her and forming man in Her own womb. Only Mary has this privilege among all created by God. She not only possesses the attributes, which the Angels have in parts in full within Her, She possesses also the Giver of these attributes in real and concrete way. You can now understand why the demon (*Professional*) could not stand Her.

While Mary lived on earth, the fullness of Her human virtues – ardent charity, profound humility, divine purity, blind obedience, lively faith, heroic patience, angelic sweetness, divine wisdom, universal mortification and continual prayer – radiate Her creaturely perfection which no other human being possess like Her. Now in heaven, She is the plenitude of every Angelic strand of grace uniting all in one unique divine handiwork: the quintessence of divine beauty and perfection:

1. She is the *Flame* of divine charity or love – *Seraphic*
2. She is the only One who best *Knows* Her Son (God) – *Cherubic*
3. She is the *Splendour* of God – a Throne of grace
4. She is crowned with Stars of *Powers*
5. She is the *Righteous One* among the Virtuous
6. She is the Queen of all *Dominions*
7. She is the *First* of the elect – Principle of all creation
8. She is the Mistress of the *Archangels*
9. She is the Queen of *Angels*.

It means that Mary has all the graces with Her. She dispenses it according to Her will, which already is intimately united with Her son's will. She can sing praises to God with Her whole being that had been dedicated to praise God naturally in the company of the first hierarchy. She can interact with nature to bring it to the original intention of the Most High in the company of the second hierarchy because She remains the only un-cursed and unstained Dust from which the second Adam took flesh to save the fallen creation. With the third hierarchy, She mostly cares for human being especially the Church, which has become part of Her son's body.

Just like the Archangels have the privilege of running through the ranks while performing their duties, Mary even more has been granted the highest privilege of being the Queen Mother of the Angels and Archangels. SHE IS HIGHLY FAVOURED!

This might help you to understand why the honour given to her by the Church (especially Catholics) is higher than that given to the Angels. Honour to the Angels is *dulia*, while honour to Mary is *hyper-dulia*. The triumphant Church in heaven honours Her so. The suffering Church in Purgatory does the same. The militant Church here on earth joins this spiritual fraternity in honouring Mary whom the Most Holy Trinity first honoured:

- She is the *Daughter* of Sion – of the Father
- The *Mother* of the Son – also of the Son's Body, the Church.
- The *Spouse* of the Holy Spirit.

If anyone is thinking that the gift God gave to Mary or the testimony I am giving of Her here is theological jargon, well and good. Just as Joshua told his brethren to decide whom to follow (cf Josh 24:15-17), as for him and his household, they will follow the Lord whose hand has clearly separated them from the other nations. Likewise, the Mother who has granted me such unmerited favour and protection since my childhood, I will join our brethren above in honouring Her as much as I can no matter how little.

In conclusion, what the Angels can do for you, the QUEEN OF ANGELS can do even more because She is endowed more to give to Her children. As we solicit the help and assistance of the Holy Messengers of God, so should we solicit for the love, care and provision of Mary, our Mother and our Queen!

APPENDIX – BELIEVERS' GUIDE

I believe someone out there after reading this might be thinking of how to start relating well with God through his or her Angel(s). I know God has been waiting for this moment to start something in your life. It is God who through His graces and sacraments first reaches out (reveals) to us always, if He does not, it would be very difficult for us to reach God. We do not think of God unless He is thinking of us, we do not love Him unless He is loving us already (Jn 4:19), we do not know Him unless he reveals Himself to us (Heb. 1:1-2) and no one comes to God unless drawn by Him (Jn 6:44). In the same way, God's mercies and kindness come to us not because we merited or worked for it but because it is already the Divine Will to bless us with all the heavenly riches in Christ (Eph. 1:3), one of these riches is the friendship and company of the holy Angels.

However, God requires our good dispositions and stewardship of these riches. It would be nice to suggest few of such disposition and stewardship that could enhance fruitful relationship with our Angels. Among other things that it might please God to personally place in your heart as divine illumination as you read this book, (for we believe more in what God does uniquely with each person than what we learn from each other), I believe PURITY, HUMILITY and LOVE OF GOD are essential virtues that attract the Holy Angels to a person. Of course, here would never be a possible forum to exhaust or fully explain these Angelic virtues.

Purity

St. Josemaria Escriva explains that *purity* makes one live like Angels in the midst of the world. The world is full of impurity and how could one resist the forces of impurity to remain pure? St. Josemaria asked the question; to defend yourself from the forces of impurity around you, what would you do? He cited examples of what the holy saints did: "*Saint Francis of Assisi rolled in the snow, Saint Benedict threw himself into a thornbush, Saint Bernard plunged into an icy pond . . . You . . . what have you done?*" St. Escriva prescribes what he called a "crusade of manliness" to fight off the assaults of impurity surging from the fire of pleasure in human flesh.

Generally many think that only sex outside lawful marriage makes one impure. Purity that is Angelic is whole and complete. St. Paul told the Church at Thessalonica that the wholeness to which the God of Peace has called them is to be *blameless, spotless* in body, soul and spirit (2 Th 5:23) at the coming of Jesus Christ. Purity in body means avoiding all that would soil the person from the concupiscence of the senses (internal and external – everything that generates in a soul, passion of lust, 1 Thes 4:5; evil desires and coveting, Rom 7:8, Col. 3:5 and libidinous appetite for worldliness like the Sodomites, Gen 19:1-11). It means dispossessing oneself of all accessories and occasions to impurity: "*sexual immorality, impurity, sensuality, idolatry, sorcery, enmity, strife, jealousy, fits of anger, rivalries, dissensions, divisions, envy, drunkenness, orgies, and things like these*" (Gal 5:19-22). These things defile the body and make it uncomfortable for our Guardian Angels and unfit for the Holy Spirit of God. St. Paul advised Timothy as a son to "flee youthful passions and pursue righteousness, faith, love and peace, along with those who call on the Lord from a *pure heart*" (2 Tim 2:22). I do not know any other who truly and completely calls on the Lord from a pure heart more than the Holy Angels. So when one strives to keep his body, soul and spirit pure, he attracts the Holy Angels. St. Don Bosco use to tell his boys "*Holy Purity, the queen of virtues, the angelic virtue, is a jewel so precious that those who possess it become like the angels of God in heaven, even though clothed in mortal flesh*".

In fact, we damage so much what we cherish and think of nothing but a passing pleasure. Think of what the Guardian Angels of two young lustful lovers will be doing the moment both engage in destroying the dwelling of the Holy Spirit and the Holy Angels. The passion of lust so much blur the reason from knowing what it really wants. Who cares! The whole wild world is aflame with lust for carnal pleasure – the internet, the Television advertisement, the fashion world, the cosmetics and even the paramedics and the medics, all vie for what attracts as *sexy* (not to the wife or husband) but to every lustful eye out there. That was why St. John Chrysostom (c. 347-407) lamented, when we would think the world was still clean, to buyers and sellers of carnal pleasures:

> *You carry your snare everywhere and spread your nets in all places. You allege that you never invited others to sin. You did not indeed, by your words, but you have done so by your dress and your deportment. ... When you have made another sin in his heart, how can you be innocent? Tell me, whom does this world condemn?*

Whom do judges punish? Those who drink poison or those who prepare it and administer the fatal potion? You have prepared the abominable cup, you have given the death dealing drink, and you are more criminal than are those who poison the body; you murder not the body but the soul. And it is not to enemies you do this, nor are you urged on by any imaginary necessity, nor provoked by injury, but out of foolish vanity and pride.

If only my senses and reason will be drained from the stupor and alcoholic hangover of transient pleasures and seek for true happiness and joy that comes from a pure life. St. Thomas Aquinas rightly observed that in matters of temptation and sin, nothing induces to sin like "thought that concern the pleasure of the flesh". It intoxicates the mind and blurs it from knowing what is good for the self. The good news for all of us is that whenever a person begins to desire purity, and doggedly applies the self (in a manly way) through *constant* or *fervent* prayer and mortification from the lustful pleasures, that person is readily assisted by their Angels to win the war because that is exactly what the Holy Angels want their wards to do for them (the Angels) to remain close to their wards. LUST AND IMPURITY DISTANCES THE ANGELS FROM THEIR WARDS. The true picture is that impurity creates huge distance between the Angels and their ward and makes inaudible their voices and inspirations to the soul. Holy purity is a gift of grace granted to every soul that earnestly desire to do God's will in all things.

Humility

Humility is the humus soil (rich and fertile ground) where purity and other virtues grow in the life of a believer and a wayfarer (pilgrim soul). Pride is the source of impurity. Lucifer was the purest flame of divine love and light. But was cast down from that height because of pride (cf. Is 14: 12-17). Lucifer, Satan or the Devil today generates all sorts of impurity as mortal bait to the carnal man. His singular means of resisting grace and God is to believe only in himself and not in God. His followers also believe more in themselves than God, Angel, Church or grace. What could make a person not to believe in something beautiful, holy and good? The Devil or Pride – both are synonymous. A proud person does not judge thing by any standard except the standard determined by him. He is the beginning and end of everything. Whatever displeasures him, discomforts him or disagrees with him does not matter much to him. This is exactly what makes the proud not to believe in God. "God", on His part, as wrote St. James, "resists the proud but gives grace to the humble" (Jm 4:6). St. Augustine remarked that "It was pride that changed Angels into devils, it is humility that makes men as Angels". The first sign of humility in any soul, as St. Louis de Blois taught, is the fear of God. That was why the Jesuit Founder, St. Ignatius of Loyola, teaches the members that,

> There is no doubt that God will never be wanting to us, provided that He finds in us that humility which makes us worthy of His gifts, the desire of possessing them, and the promptitude to co-operate industriously with the graces He gives us.

What a noble gift of grace the Angels are to wretched beings like us! Only pride can blind one from believing in them, let alone soliciting for their help. Let the same mind that was in our Lord Jesus Christ be in you, St. Paul counseled the Philipians (cf. 2:5). Jesus was of equal status and power with God but he humbled himself and obeyed the Father's Will to a shameful end. For this God exalted Him and graced Him above everything. The Angels ministered to Jesus even when He has left the tomb (Mtt. 28:1-7; Mk. 16:2-7; Lk 24:1-8). Any Pilgrim or Wayfarer who humbles himself to do God's will can never be without the helpful presence of Holy Messengers of God. Hebrew 1:14 resonates the question: "*Are not Angels ministering Spirits sent to serve them who shall inherit salvation?*" Yes, they are sent after you and after me to assist us reach our eternal happiness! Whoever humbly accepts this, already receives and opens up to their ministry.

Love of God

"*The Lord looks down from heaven* (searches the heart) *upon men to see if any are wise, if any seek God...*" (Ps 53: 2).

What attracts the Angels most in any person is the love of God. A heart that sincerely searches for God, a heart that truly longs for his God (Ps 42: 2), attracts the Holy Angels like a bright light attracts moths in a dark night. The Holy Messengers of God have made a decisive and resolute commitment to serve the *Divine Will*. They are automatically united with every human heart that earnestly seeks to live for and serve the same Divine Will.

Therefore, if anyone really desires special company and help of these Holy Messengers, he or she should surely pray to have a heart that seeks and loves to please God. Sincere love of God is what we found common in all the saints whose lives were favoured with extraordinary friendship with the Angels. WHAT ANGELS LOVE MOST IN MEN ARE LOVE OF GOD, PURITY AND HUMILITY.

Communication/Prayer

First of all every communication requires giving and receiving; or speaker and the listener; or give and take inform of bilateral exchange. Communication is never one ended. No body makes a call with one ended telephone. There must be someone on the other end to pick the call. That means, God, Holy Spirit or Angels, must be realities concretely existing in the persons mind. They cannot be probable figments of the mind. Or some doctrinally inherited spiritual images that are not real or actual. Communication begins when there are two or more concrete, real and actual persons in the interaction.

Angels are spiritual beings that are not subject to *spatio*-temporal limitations. Like God, they love human beings and are always ready to serve us according to divine biddings. Just as the Holy Spirit of God works through our own 'spirit' (cf. Rm 8:6) and bears 'witness' to the TRUTH about LIFE (cf 1Jn 5:6-8), likewise the Holy Messengers communicate through the *spirit* of those who believe in them illumining their mind, soul and intellect with the right *Way* to follow, the *Truth* to believe in and the *Life* to embrace. Through their celestial light, the Angels directly and interiorly communicate to the soul of their wards. They also communicate externally using available external instrument to reach the attention of the ward as in the case of Balaam and his donkey (Num 22:22-35 or cf. Paul's case in Act 16:6-7).

Angels can take human form to visit and communicate to us like they did to Abraham and other Patriarchs we listed above. They can communicate through our godly intuitions and flash of instant awareness or knowledge of divine plans hidden or forgotten in our memories (cf. Eph. 3:1-6). In some cases, they use dreams (Mt. 1:20, 2:19) and visions (Lk 2:9; Acts 5:19; 6:15, etc) as permitted by God's ordering. But the right way to know that it is the Holy Angels and not impostors as 'angel of the light' communicating is to watch the fruit. You know them by their fruit (Mt. 7:16). If Angels are concrete Messengers in our life, they must be communicating in

141

some way to us. No one can actually say all the possible ways they could communicate. As individuals and persons are unique, so also Angels communicate to their wards according to their unique circumstances. But surely Angels communicate to their ward.

The problem is: *does the ward pick up their call* when it is wringing. And if he picks, does he understand the language. And when he understands the language, is he ready to respond and obey? This is where prayer and quiet moments are practically indispensable for active persons. Just as babies know their mother first through feeling (sensory knowledge) and later through recognition (cognitive knowledge), so every true prayer begins from the heart and is affirmed by the mind or intellect. A ritual prayer that does not touch the heart or our feelings ends in ideals that are not real. Likewise emotional prayers that are only sensual and not reasonable end up in carnal satisfaction, like spiritual opium to relieve the carnal desires. Hence, communication in prayer should not be one way. A prayer recited to an unknown God is like a letter posted without address. It does not get to any place. Nor, can the word of God, the sacraments and fellowship of the holy assemblies where God is worshipped be received attended without personal response of the individual. Relationship with Angels would be the same. Communication from the believer's heart nourished and aided by rites and holy sacraments and assemblies (fellowship or worship) elicits a response from the Messengers and vice versa.

In the negative or occult world, there are sanctuaries, both personal or familial or communal dedicated to some monitoring or personal demons. Those sanctuaries are always a good meeting place between the ward and the demon. But believers presume that their Holy Angels do not need a quiet place, be it sanctuary, haven, harbor, Church, or altar to communicate. St. James exhorted his congregation strongly that the nearer you draw to God, the nearer God draws to you (Jm 4:8). One who personalizes his Angel(s) like Padre Pio and even gives him (them) personal pal name(s), is more likely to reap the fruit of their presence than one who tolerates them as figures of religious imagination. WHY NOT TRY REACHING TO YOUR ANGEL, HE HAS BEEN WAITING FOR SO LONG!

PART THREE – DEVOTION TO THE ANGELS

Here we would like to suggest some traditional devotional prayers. The prayers will be grouped into three: some prayers of Angels to the Almighty; some prayers to the Angels and, praying with Angels for various needs.

SOME PRAYERS OF THE ANGELS TO THE ALMIGHTY

1. *Angelic Praises of God and Jesus in the Blessed Sacrament*

   Holy, Holy, Holy Lord God of Hosts!
   Heaven and Earth are full of thy Glory
   Praise to Thee oh Lord in the Highest!

   O Sacrament Most Holy, O Sacrament Divine!
   All Praises and all Thanksgiving be every moment Thine!

2. *Prayer taught by the Angels of Portugal to the three Little Kids*

   My God, I believe, I adore, I hope, and I love You.   I ask pardon for those who do not believe,   do not adore, do not hope, and do not love You.

SOME PRAYERS TO THE ANGELS

1.   *Prayer to the Queen of Angels*

A Bernardine Sister was shown in spirit the vast desolation caused by the devil throughout the world, and at the same time she heard the Blessed Virgin telling her that it was true, hell had been let loose upon the earth; and that the time had come to pray to her as Queen of the Angels and to ask of her the assistance of the heavenly legions to fight against these deadly foes of God and of men.

"But my good Mother," she replied, "you who are so kind, could you not send them without our asking?" "No," Our Lady answered, "because prayer is one of the conditions required by God Himself in obtaining favors." Then the Blessed Virgin communicated the following prayer, bidding the Sister to have it printed and distributed:

August Queen of Heaven! Sovereign Mistress of the angels! Thou who from the beginning hast received from God the power and mission to crush the head of Satan, we humbly beseech thee to send thy holy Legions, that, under thy command and by thy power, they may pursue the evil spirits, encounter them on every side, resist their bold attacks and drive them hence into the abyss of eternal woe. Amen.

2.   *Prayer for Angelic Assistance*

Lord Almighty, Creator of all life, thank You for creating the Angels.

As dedicated and faithful Servants, they instantly act upon Your commands.

Please direct Your Angels to assist me, ensuring the accomplishment of Your work,

In accordance with Your Divine will. Always rekindle my mind to remember

That Your angels are available to me as restrainers of diabolic obstacles.

Thank You Lord for Your auspice! Your kindness is infinitely good!

3. *Request to the Nine Choirs!*

Bless the Lord, All you His Angels, You who are Mighty in strength and do His Will.

Intercede for me at the throne of God, and by your unceasing watchfulness protect me in every danger of soul and body.

Obtain for me the grace of final perseverance, So that after this life I may be admitted to your glorious company and may sing with you the praises of God for all eternity.

O all you holy Angels And Archangels, Thrones and Dominations, Principalities and Powers And Virtues of heaven, Cherubim and Seraphim And especially you, my dear Guardian Angel, Intercede for me and obtain for me the special favor I now ask

(State your intention here...).

Say 9 Our Father...

4. *Prayer to Archangel Michael for Personal Protection*

St. Michael, the Archangel! Glorious Prince, chief and champion of the heavenly hosts; guardian of the souls of men; conqueror of the rebel angels! How beautiful art thou, in thy heaven-made armor. We love thee, dear Prince of Heaven!

> We, thy happy clients, yearn to enjoy thy special protection. Obtain for us from God a share of thy sturdy courage; pray that we may have a strong and tender love for our Redeemer and, in every danger or temptation, be invincible against the enemy of our souls. O standard-bearer of our salvation! Be with us in our last moments and when our souls quit this earthly exile, carry them safely to the judgement seat of Christ, and may Our Lord and Master bid thee bear us speedily to the kingdom of eternal bliss. Teach us ever to repeat the sublime cry: "Who is like unto God?" Amen.

5. *Prayer to St Michael Against Spiritual Enemies*

Glorious St. Michael, Prince of the heavenly hosts, who stands always ready to give assistance to the people of God; who fought with the dragon, the old serpent, and cast him out of heaven, and now valiantly defends the Church of God that the gates of hell may never prevail against her, I earnestly entreat thee to assist me also, in the painful and dangerous conflict which I have to sustain against the same formidable foe. Be with me, O mighty Prince! That I may courageously fight and wholly vanquish that proud spirit, whom thou by the Divine Power, so gloriously overthrown, and whom our powerful King, Jesus Christ, has, in our nature, so completely overcome; to the end that having triumphed over the enemy of my salvation, I may with thee and the holy angels, praise the clemency of God who, having refused mercy to the rebellious angels after their fall, has granted repentance and forgiveness to fallen man. Amen.

6. *Prayer to St. Raphael for a Happy Meeting*

O Raphael, lead us towards those we are waiting for, those who are waiting for us! Raphael, Angel of Happy Meetings, lead us by the hand towards those we are looking for! May all our movements, all their movements, be guided by your Light and transfigured by your Joy.

Angel Guide of Tobias, lay the request we now address to you at the feet of Him on whose unveiled Face you are privileged to gaze. Lonely and tired, crushed by the separations and sorrows of earth, we feel the need of calling to you and of pleading for the protection of your wings, so that we may not be as strangers in the Province of Joy, all ignorant of the concerns of our country.

7. *Prayer to St. Gabriel for Intercession*

O Blessed Archangel Gabriel, we beseech thee, do thou intercede for us at the throne of divine Mercy in our present necessities, that as thou didst announce to Mary the mystery of the Incarnation, so through thy prayers and patronage in heaven we may obtain the benefits of the same, and sing the praise of God forever in the land of the living. Amen.

8. *Prayer to the Angel that Strengthened Jesus at Gethsamene for support in Difficult Moments*

I salute thee, holy Angel who didst comfort my Jesus in His agony, and with thee I praise the most holy Trinity for having chosen thee from among all the holy Angels to comfort and strengthen Him who is the comfort and strength of all that are in affliction. By the honor thou didst enjoy and by the obedience, humility and love wherewith thou didst assist the sacred Humanity of Jesus, my Savior, when He was fainting for very sorrow at seeing the sins of the world and especially my sins, I beseech thee to obtain for me perfect sorrow for my sins; deign to strengthen me In the afflictions that now overwhelm me, and in all the other trials, to which I shall be exposed henceforth and, in particular, when I find myself in my final agony. Amen.

9. *General Prayer to all the Guardian Angels*

O pure and happy spirits whom the Almighty selected to become the Angels and Guardians of men. I most humbly prostrate myself before thee to thank thee for the charity and zeal with which thou dost execute this commission. Alas, how many pass a long life without ever thanking their invisible friends, to whom they owe a thousand times their preservation!

O charitable Guardians of those souls for whom Christ died, O flaming spirits, who cannot avoid loving those whom Jesus eternally loved, permit me to address thee on behalf of all those committed to thy care, to implore for each of them a grateful sense of thine many favors and also the grace to profit by thine charitable assistance.

O Angels of those happy infants who are as yet "without spot before God," I earnestly beseech thee to preserve their innocence.

O Angels of youth, conduct them, exposed to so many dangers, safely to the bosom of God, as Tobias was conducted back to his father.

O Angels of those who employ themselves in the instruction of youth, animate them with thy zeal and love, teach them to emulate thy purity and continual view of God, that they may worthily and successfully co-operate with the invisible Guardians of their young charges.

O Angels of the clergy, of those "who have the eternal Gospel to preach to them that sit upon the earth," present their words, their actions and their intentions to God,

and purify them in that fire of love that consumes thee. O Angels of the missionaries who have left their native land and all who were dear to them in order to preach the Gospel in foreign fields, protect them from the dangers which threaten them, console in their hours of discouragement and solitude, and lead them to those souls who are in danger of dying without Baptism.

O Angels of the infidels and pagans, whom the True Faith has never enlightened, intercede for them, that they may open their hearts to the rays of grace, respond to the message delivered by God's missioners and acknowledge and adore the one true God.

O Angels of all who travel by air, land or water, be their guides and companions, protect them from all dangers of collision, fire, and explosion and lead them safely to their destination.

O Guardian Angels of sinners, charitable guides of those unhappy mortals whose perseverance in sin would embitter even thine unutterable joys, wert thou not established in the peace of God! Oh join me, I ardently beseech thee, in imploring their conversion!

And thou, O Guardian Angels of the sick, I entreat thee especially to help, console and implore the spirits of joy for all those who are deprived of health, which is among God's most precious gifts to man. Intercede for them, that they may not succumb to despondency or lose by impatience the merits they can gain in carrying with resignation and joy the cross which Christ has laid upon them as a special token of His love.

O Angels of those are at this moment in the agonies of death, strengthen, encourage and defend them against the attacks of their infernal enemy.

O faithful Guides, holy spirits, adorers of the Divinity, Guardian Angels of all creatures, protect us all; teach us to love, to pray, to wage combat on earth, so that one day we may reach Heaven and there be happy for all eternity!

Amen.

> O Angels of those who are lingering in Purgatory, intercede for them that God may permit thee to bring them some balm; console them that they may know that we are praying for them and that we ask thee to join in our entreaties.

10. *Thanksgiving to my Guardian Angel*

O Angel of God, my blessed protector, to whose care I have been committed by my Creator from the moment of my birth, unite with me in thanking the Almighty for having given me a friend, and instructor, an advocate, and a guardian in thee.

Accept, O most charitable guide, my fervent thanksgiving for all thou hast done for me; particularly for the charity with which thou didst undertake to accompany me through life; for the joy with which thou wert filled when I was purified in the waters of Baptism; and for thy anxious solicitude in watching over the treasure of my innocence.

Thou knowest the numberless graces and favors which my Creator has bestowed on me through thee, and the many dangers, both spiritual and temporal from which thou hast preserved me.

Thou knowest how often thou didst deplore my sins, animate me to repentance, and intercede with God for my pardon.

Ah! why have I so little merited a continuance of thy zealous efforts for my salvation?

Why have I so often stained my soul by sin, and thereby rendered myself unworthy of the presence and protection of an angel, of so pure a spirit as thou art, who never sinned?

But as my ingratitude and thoughtlessness have not lessened thy charitable interest for my salvation, so neither shall they diminish my confidence in thy goodness, nor prevent me from abandoning myself to thy care, since God Himself has entrusted thee with the charge of my soul.

Penetrated with sorrow for the little progress I have made in virtue, though blessed with such a Master, and sincerely determined to correspond in future with thy exertions for my salvation, I most earnestly entreat thee, O protecting spirit, to continue thy zealous efforts for my eternal interest; to fortify my weakness, to shield me from innumerable dangers of the world and to obtain by thy powerful prayers that my life may rather be shortened, than that I should live to commit a mortal sin.

Remember, O most happy spirit, that it was one act of profound humility, and one transport of ardent love for thy Creator, that caused God to establish thee forever in glory; obtain that those virtues may be implanted in my soul, and that I may seriously endeavor to acquire docility, obedience, gentleness and purity of heart.

Conduct me safely through this world of sin and misery; watch over me at the awful hour of my death; perform for my soul the last charitable office of thy mission, by strengthening, encouraging, and supporting me in the agonies of dissolution, and then, as the angel Raphael conducted Tobias safely to his father, do thou, my good angel and blessed guide, return with me to Him who sent thee, that we may mutually bless Him, and publish His wonderful works for a happy eternity.

Amen.

11. *Prayer to the Guardian Angel when Unable to Assist at Mass*

Go, my Angel Guardian dear, To church for me, the Mass to hear. Go, kneel devoutly at my place And treasure for me every grace. At the Offertory time Please offer me to God Divine. All I have and all I am, Present it with the Precious Lamb. Adore for me the great Oblation. Pray for all I hold most dear Be they far or be they near. Rmember too, my own dear dead For whom Christ's Precious Blood was shed. And at Communion bring to me Christ's Flesh and Blood, my food to be. To give me strength and holy grace A pledge to see Him face to face And when the Holy Mass is done Then with His blessing, come back home.

12. *Mamma's Prayer to the Guardian Angels of her children*

I humbly salute you, O you faithful, heavenly Friends of my children! I give you heartfelt thanks for all the love and goodness you show them. At some future day I shall, with thanks more worthy than I can now give, repay your care for them, and before the whole heavenly court acknowledge their indebtedness to your guidance and protection. Continue to watch over them. Provide for all their needs of body and soul. Pray, likewise, for me, for my husband, and my whole family, that we may all one day rejoice in your blessed company. Amen.

CALLING ON THE ANGELS FOR VARIOUS NEEDS

1. *Angels of Faith for Strong Faith in God*

Oh you *faithful Servants* of the Most High, obtain for me from the heavenly throne of grace a renewal of my baptismal gift of Faith. Make my Faith in God strong and undivided. Faith based not on my feelings but on the revealed truths in Jesus Christ; Faith that is simple and unpresumptuous, docile to the testimony of Holy Spirit and expectant of the joys of everlasting life, Amen.

2. *Angels of Love for Selfless Love*

Oh you heavenly flames of Divine Love, inflame my heart with ardent love for God and neighbour; that I may always hold God dear above everything around me.
Open my eyes that I may see people around me from the radiant light of your *seraphic* love. Heat my lukewarm heart in the embers of your angelic love that I may be stable and not vacillate between the true love of God and worldly love. Make my heart like the heart of Jesus and Mary, always ready and willing to die in obedience to divine commands and totally submissive to His Will, Amen.

3. *Angels of Hope not to Despair*

Oh you untiring Holy Messengers of Hope, bearers of the Good News! You know how much I need hope when I am helpless and despairing: when all seems gloomy and dark. Come to me always with your rays of light and hope to strengthen my trembling kneels and to steady my wobbling faith. Sustain my hope for the joys of heaven that I may never give up in doing what is right amidst the passing sufferings of the present moment. May your comfort guard me still till I reach the everlasting pasture that never withers, Amen.

4. *Angels of Reconciliation when Fallen into Sin*

Oh you holy intercessors surrounding the throne of Divine Mercy, as it is the Will of the Most High that I should not continue to be clad in the filthy garments of my failures (Zach 3: 1-5), help me to recognize my shortcomings and to truly own them without excuses. Obtain for me genuine contrition for my failures so that I may be more determined by your ever-friendly assistance to overcome them in the future.

Dispose me by your humble prayers to be ready to understand and assist with tenderness those who are weak and broken-hearted due to habitual failures. Never allow me to remain complacent with any sin or error that will separate me from the grace and love of God. Fill my soul with horror for sin no matter how little, Amen.

5.   *Angels of Conversion*

Oh Holy Messengers of conversion, with your overpowering light you struck Saul and turned him into St. Paul. I pray that by the merits of the masses celebrated throughout the altars of the world and in union with the prayers and sacrifices of the saints rising up to the throne of His Majesty at this moment you may search out and turn agents of darkness into agents of light, carriers of hatred and wickedness into carriers of love and goodness. Bring sinners on the path of righteousness and save souls from eternal perdition, Amen.

6.   *Angels of Deliverance*

I invoke you Holy Principalities and Powers of heaven, descend with the warring armaments of heaven into the dungeons, temples, covens, shrines, infernal kingdoms and other unnamed diabolic prisons and enclosures. With the victory of Jesus Christ of Nazareth at whose name every kneel bows (Phil 2:10); with the victory in His blood which ransoms men for God from every tribe and people and nation (Rev 5:9), with the glory of His resurrection which commands every ancient chain, keys or gates to open on its own (Ps 24:9), and with the His consuming Flame which goes before Him to devour His foes on every side (Ps 97:3), free every human soul of all foreign (diabolic) emblems or identity.

Free every child of God who still believes in God but has fallen into the captivity of the evil one from all their imprisonments.

Free those tormented by fear of the evil forces from the terrors of these infernal demons and de-covenant those tied to all forms of soulish bondages/covenants through the power of the new covenant in the precious blood of Jesus Christ.

Destroy all that the enemy uses to frustrate the children of God from living a righteous life – spirit of pride, lust, licentiousness, drunkenness, anger, greed, sloth, idolatry, occultism and similar vices – and purify their souls to be clean of the debris of these evil works.

Rise up Holy warriors of heaven and set the children redeemed in the precious Blood of Jesus from all evil. When the Son of man sets you free, you are free indeed (Jn 8:36). May the children of God, through your agency be free to worship God in holiness and righteousness all the days of their life (Lk 1:73) in Jesus' Name, Amen.

7. ***Angels of Healing** for Spiritual and Corporal Health*

I implore thee Archangel Raphael and all the healing Angels of God, especially the Angels that stirs up the Sacred Wounds of Jesus for healing like you stirred up the pool of Bethzatha. Touch my.... (*Mention the sickness or touch the place to be healed with your right hand*) with the Healing Blood from Jesus' Holy Wounds, cast out from me all spirits of infirmity as Raphael did to Asmodeus and send them to their proper places. Fill my ailing spirit and body with the healing power of the Holy Spirit, anointing me afresh with the soothing Balm of Gilead so that I may be fully restored to complete health in body, soul and spirit.

Holy healing Agents of heaven! Pray down the healing Power of the Holy Spirit so that I may through my nostrils now breath-in healing and release-out all the ailments in my entire *psycho-somatic* spiritual system.

Healing Spirits of God, "the life of a thing is in its blood" (Lev 17:11) make my bones, tissue, veins, nerves and all the organic fluids in my body to be renewed with the Life that flows from the Precious Blood of Jesus now. He was wounded that I may be healed (Is 53: 5). Through the Mercy of the Crucified Jesus, take away this ... (*mention again*) ailment that I may be free from it.

With all the Angels of God, I will always praise and thanks the Lord for His mercies, proclaiming His Goodness to me all the days of my life (Ps 145)!

8. ***Angels of Protection...***

Oh you Holy Angels commanded by the Most High to guard me in all my ways (Ps 91:11), protect me from all the evil plans the foul spirits have against me today and all the days of my life. Watch over my path that I may not fall into any accident or misfortune placed on my pathway by the enemy (human or demonic). He never sleeps nor slumbers the Guardian of His people (Ps 121:3)! Be at alert over my entire spiritual and material well being that I may dwell under your ever protective and watchful care. Never allow the sun or moon of unrighteousness to shine over me. Lead me out and bring me home safely always. May all my good plans and purposes be accomplished under your protection through Jesus Christ our Lord, Amen.

9. *Angels of Blessings/Favour...*

Oh Archangel Gabriel and all you Holy Angels of God that carry the Good News of Blessings and favour from the Most High, intercede on my behalf as you did for Daniel (Dan 10). Bring favourable answers to my prayers that I may like Sarah be visited with fruitfulness over my past bareness (Gen 18), like Jacob that I may an over comer in every battle that will change my lot and my identity for good (Gen 31), like Mary I may be highly favoured (Lk 1:28) in whatever I undertake. Receive for me from the bounty of the Most High, unimaginable riches that will make my spiritual and temporal journey bearable. May I be a giver and not a receiver in every good work. Make me a blessing not only to myself and my own but to all I meet, Amen.

10. Angels of Break-through...

Oh Holy Servants of the Most High, you that waits on God always to accomplish His bidding (the unemployed Ones), in the name of Jesus Christ who assures me that whatever I ask in His name will be granted (Jn 13:14) I employ you now to go before me to accomplish this new task... (mention the new task you are undertaking). Obtain for me the constancy and steadfastness to work hard and to remain in prayers without losing heart (Lk 18) till this task is accomplished to the glory of God. Do not allow the devourers to scatter what have been done but keep me confident and resolute to the end (1 Thes 5:17) till people give God all the praise for such a wonderful achievement in my life. My God is the One to whom nothing is impossible, I believe with you by my side, I can achieve anything granted to me already from above.